Men-at-Arms • 356

Armies in the Balkans 1914–18

Nigel Thomas Ph.D. & Dusan Babac • Illustrated by Darko Pavlovic

Series editor Martin Windrow

First published in Great Britain in 2001 by Osprey Publishing,
Midland House, West Way, Botley, Oxford OX2 0PH, UK
44-02 23rd St, Suite 219, Long Island City, NY 11101, USA
E-mail: info@ospreypublishing.com

Transferred to digital print on demand 2010

First published 2001
6th impression 2008

Printed and bound in Great Britain

A CIP catalogue record for this book is available from the British Library

ISBN: 978 1 84176 194 7

Series Editor: Martin Windrow
Editorial by Anita Hitchings
Design by Alan Hamp
Index by Alan Rutter
Rank-charts by Darko Pavlovic
Originated by Colourpath, London, UK

Dedication

This book is respectfully dedicated to Dusan Babac's late grandfather, Major (retired) Pavle Babac, former commander of the 1st
Battalion, 2nd 'Prince Mihailo' 'Iron' Regiment of the Royal Yugoslav Army.

Acknowledgements

This book would not have been possible without the generous help of many people. Nigel Thomas would like to thank Krunoslav
Mikulan, Darko Pavlovic, Philip Jowett, Horia Serbanescu, Lt. Cdr. (ret) Maitland Thornton; also his wife Heather and sons Alexander
and Dominick. Dusan Babac would like to thank Predrag-Preza Milosavljevic, Cedomir Vasic, Milan Markovic, Branko Bogdanovic;
also his parents, wife Olja and son Vukasin for their support.

Author's Note

Throughout this text we follow British practice in using the term 'Other Ranks' to mean enlisted, non-officer personnel; and
international prcatice in using e.g. 'M1915' to identify all dated patterns of clothing and equipment.

Artist's Note

Readers may care to note that the original paintings from which the colour plates in this book were prepared are available for private
sale. All reproduction copyright whatsoever is retained by the Publishers. All enquiries should be addressed to:
Darko Pavlovic,
Modecova 3,
10090 Zagreb,
Croatia.
The Publishers regret that they can enter into no correspondence upon this matter.

MIX
Paper from
responsible sources
FSC® C013604

FOR A CATALOGUE OF ALL BOOKS PUBLISHED BY OSPREY
MILITARY AND AVIATION PLEASE CONTACT:

Osprey Direct, c/o Random House Distribution Center,
400 Hahn Road, Westminster, MD 21157
Email: uscustomerservice@ospreypublishing.com

Osprey Direct, The Book Service Ltd, Distribution Centre,
Colchester Road, Frating Green, Colchester, Essex, CO7 7DW
E-mail: customerservice@ospreypublishing.com

www.ospreypublishing.com

ARMIES IN THE BALKANS 1914-18

THE BALKAN CAMPAIGN

Todor Stavric, Dusan Babac's great-grandfather, as a private *(Infanterist)* in a Bosnian Infantry Regiment relaxing in walking-out dress, 1914. He wears the M1908 pike-grey tunic with red branch-colour collar patches, standard (not baggy Bosnian) M1908 trousers, and long socks instead of puttees; although he was a Serbian Orthodox Christian, a plain crimson service dress fez; M1888 belt with Austrian eagle buckle, and M1895 bayonet with Other Ranks' knot. (Dusan Babac Collection)

IN 1914 THE BALKAN PENINSULA comprised 258,000 square miles with about 26 million inhabitants: Albanians, Bulgarians, Greeks, Rumanians, South Slavs – Serbs (including Montenegrins), Bosnian Moslems, Croats (including Dalmatians) and Slovenes – with German, Hungarian, Italian, Jewish, Vlach and other minorities. These peoples had just emerged from 568 years of occupation by the Ottoman Turks, and lived in Albania, Bulgaria, Greece, Montenegro, Rumania and Serbia (including present-day Macedonia); with Bosnia-Herzegovina, Croatia and Slovenia under Austro-Hungarian rule. The European remnant of the Ottoman Empire comprised the capital Constantinople, Edirne and their hinterlands.

The Balkans, whose violent instability had earned the region the title of the 'powder-keg of Europe', were marked by the rivalry between German-backed Austro-Hungary, ambitious to control the region; and Serbia, supported by Russia and France, which was determined to liberate Serb, Croat, Slovene and Bosnian minorities in Austro-Hungary. Meanwhile Bulgaria was anxious to regain areas in Greek and Serbian Macedonia and Rumanian Dobrudja, forfeited in August 1913 following the Second Balkan War.

Austro-Hungary had provoked Serbia by holding military manoeuvres in Bosnia-Herzegovina in summer 1914; and on 28 June a Bosnian-Serb student, Gavril Princip, assassinated the Austro-Hungarian Crown Prince Franz Ferdinand in Sarajevo, thus igniting the First World (or 'Great') War.

The Defence of Serbia

The four Central Powers – Germany, Austro-Hungary, the Ottoman Empire and Bulgaria – intended to link up territorially by Austro-Hungary occupying Serbia and Montenegro, and dominating Albania, leaving Greece and Rumania as benevolent neutral states. This strategy was opposed by the three principal European 'Entente' Powers – France, Great Britain and Russia.

3

The map shows the Balkans with labels including AUSTRIAN-HUNGARIAN EMPIRE, AUSTRIA, VIENNA, BUDAPEST, HUNGARY, SLOVENIA, LJUBLJANA, ZAGREB, CROATIA, SLAVONIA, TRANSYLVANIA, BANAT, BOSNIA-HERZEGOVINA, Srebrenica, SARAJEVO, Pale, Kalinovik, Foča, Mojkovac, SERBIA, BELGRADE, Loznica, Valjevo, Užice, Kragujevac, Niš, RUMANIA, WALLACHIA, BUCHAREST, Flâminda, Ruse, RUSSIAN EMPIRE, BUKOVINA, BESSARABIA, MOLDAVIA, Iaşi, Chişinăev, ODESSA, Mărăşti, Oituz, Mărăşeşti, Galaţi, DOBRUDJA, Varna, BULGARIA, SOFIA, MONTE-NEGRO, CETINJE, Bar, Shkodër, ALBANIA, TIRANË, Durrës, KOSOVO, ÜSKUB, MACEDONIA, Prilep, Monastir, Skradi, Berat, Pogradec, Korçë, SOUTH EPIRUS, Vlorë, WESTERN THRACE, Dráma, Kavála, SALONIKA, Edirne, CONSTANTINOPLE, OTTOMAN EMPIRE, GREECE, ATHENS, Corfu, Brindisi, ITALY, Adriatic Sea, Ionian Sea, Aegean Sea, Dodecanese Isles, Danube, Drava, Sava, Tisa, Morava, Kolubara, Vardar, Struma, Prut, Siret, Dniestar

BORDERS IN 1914
BORDERS AFTER 1918

OPPOSITE **Two subaltern officers of the Austro-German Defence Force's 13th Artillery Battalion, January 1915. They wear M1908 pike-grey tunics and trousers with civilian fur hats and scarves in the snowy weather. The lieutenant (Oberleutnant) on the left has brown leather dismounted officers' gaiters and ankle boots, the officer (right) Other Ranks' cavalry riding boots. Both carry M1861 infantry officers' sabres, M1907 Roth-Steyr 8mm automatic pistols with their distinctive holsters and shoulder belts, and non-standard flashlights. (Dusan Babac Collection)**

The Austro-Hungarian 'Balkan Army' – effectively an army group, comprising 2nd Army in Syrmia (Eastern Croatia) and Western Banat (now Vojvodina, Northern Serbia); 5th Army in East-Central Bosnia and Herzegovina; and 6th Army in North-Eastern Bosnia – attempted three invasions of Serbia and Montenegro. On 28 July 1914 the 2nd Army shelled Belgrade, and the first invasion began on 2 August. The 5th Army crossed the Drina into North-Western Serbia towards Belgrade, where it and the 2nd Army were defeated on 12-24 August by the Serbian 1st, 2nd and 3rd Armies at the battle of Cer (Lesnica) – the first Allied victory of the First World War.

A Serbian counterattack into Syrmia on 6 September was abandoned after the second Austro-Hungarian invasion on 8 September, when the 5th and 6th Armies again threatened Belgrade. At the battle of the Drina the Serbian 2nd Army forced the 5th Army back into Bosnia, while the 6th Army, after initial headway against the Serbian 3rd Army, also retreated to avoid a bold outflanking movement on 25 September, with the Serbian Uzice Group and Montenegrin armies advancing towards Srebrenica and Pale in Eastern Bosnia. The Serbs retreated tactically before the third Austro-Hungarian invasion on 6 November, with Serbian 2nd Army allowing the Austro-Hungarian 5th Army to occupy Belgrade on 2 December. The Austro-Hungarian 6th Army was halted before

Valjevo and defeated on 3-9 December by the Serbian 1st Army at the battle of Kolubara, before being forced back into Syrmia. Meanwhile, the regrouped Serbian 2nd and 3rd Armies and the Uzice Group drove the 5th Army into Western Banat, liberating Belgrade on 15 December 1914.

Some 20,000 Serbian troops of the 'Albanian Detachment' occupied Northern and Central Albania on 29 May 1915 to forestall cross-border raids into Kosovo and South Serbia by Albanian émigrés. This, however, weakened the main Serbian force confronting the Central Powers. On 18 September 1915 Germany established Army Group Mackensen, comprising the German 11th, Austro-Hungarian 3rd and Bulgarian 1st Armies. Then, on 5 October 1915, a Franco-British force landed in Salonika and the Austro-Hungarians entered Montenegro, capturing Mount Lovcen on 10 January 1916, Cetinje on 13th and Berat in Southern Albania on 17 February 1916. On 11 October Bulgarian forces attacked Serbia, the 1st Army taking the crucial rail junction of Nis on 5 November, reaching Elbasan in Albania, and the 2nd Army advancing along the Vardar Valley to attack beleaguered Serbo-Montenegrin forces. However, on 6 October Mackensen's 3rd and 11th Armies advanced down the Morava Valley, taking Belgrade on 8 October and Kragujevac on the 15th. As an outflanking action the Austro-Hungarian 57th, 59th and 63rd Divisions advanced from Eastern Bosnia against weak Serbian forces, occupying Üskub (now Skopje) on 22 October and brushing aside a premature Allied thrust from Salonika.

The Serbian forces now conducted their legendary tactical retreat from 24 November across snow-laden mountain passes through Kosovo and Montenegro, across the Prokletije Mountains into Northern and Central Albania and down to the Adriatic coast, leaving the Montenegrin

ABOVE **Three soldiers of the Austro-Hungarian army in the M1915 field-grey field uniform, summer 1917. The lance-corporal (Gefreiter) (left) wears a tunic with M1908 coloured collar patches, a stiffened field cap, breeches, riding boots and M1909 leather equipment. His two companions are wearing lighter-weight tunics with no collar patches or coloured collar strips, breeches and puttees. Note the soft field cap worn by the middle soldier; and the characteristic Austro-Hungarian style of holding the strap of the shouldered rifle taut. The Austro-Hungarian army had 28 per cent Austro-Germans; 44 per cent Slavs (Croats, Serbs, Slovenes, Czechs, Slovaks, Poles, Ukrainians); 18 per cent Hungarians; 8 per cent Rumanians and 2 per cent Italians. (Dusan Babac Collection)**

army to conduct a last stand before surrendering on 25 January 1916. By late December 1915 the Serbs had reached Shkodër, and on 15 January 1916 were evacuated by Allied ships from Durrës – initially to French-occupied Corfu and as far as Bizerta in French Tunisia, and from April 1916 to the Salonika Front. In January 1916 Austro-Hungary installed a military government *(Militär-Generalgouvernement)* in Serbia and Montenegro, using Gendarmerie and Military Police *(Feld-gendarmerie)* to fight local Chetnik guerrillas.

The Salonika Front

The Central Powers now controlled the Western Balkans, their forces grouped from 22 April 1917 as Army Group Scholtz. The Austro-Hungarian 19th Corps in Northern and Central Albania opposed the Italian 16th Corps on a 60-mile front in South-Western Albania. The Allied *Armée de l'Orient* deployed along the Serbian-Greek border on a 160-mile front divided into five sectors. The French 3rd Divisional Group manned the Ochrid Sector (Skumbin River–Lake Prespa) and the Franco-Russian 2nd Group the Monastir Sector (Lake Prespa–Gradesnica) against the German 11th Army. The reconstituted Serbian forces defended the Crna Sector (Gradesnica–Crna River) with 1st–3rd Serbian Armies; the Franco-Italian 1st Group the Struma Sector (Crna–Vardar Rivers); and the British Salonika Army the Doiran Sector (Vardar–Struma Rivers), against the Bulgarian 1st and 2nd Armies. In the East the neutralist Greek 4th Corps garrisoned Eastern Macedonia against the Bulgarian 2nd and 4th Armies.

Germany vetoed an Austro-Hungarian-Bulgarian attack on Salonika in order to tie down Allied forces and discourage their transfer to the Western Front. Nevertheless, at the battle of Flórina (or Gornicevo) in the Monastir and Crna Sectors, 17 August–14 September 1916, initial gains by the Bulgarian 1st Army were retaken by the 2nd Divisional Group and the Serbian 1st Army, while the Bulgarian 2nd Army forced the British Salonika Army back in the Doiran Sector during the Struma Valley operations. Meanwhile, the Greek 4th Corps, ordered by the Athens government not to resist in order to avoid compromising Greek neutrality, surrendered Fort Rupel on 24 May and on 18 September Eastern Macedonia as far as the strategic port of Kaválla, to the Bulgarian 2nd and 4th Armies. During the successful Allied counteroffensive in the Monastir and Crna Sectors (5 October–11 December 1916) Monastir (now Bitola) was captured by Serbian cavalry and Russian infantry on

Personnel from the Austro-Hungarian 2nd Assault Troops (Sturmtruppe) Company at Banja Luka, Central Bosnia-Herzogovina, May 1918. All are wearing the M1915 field tunic with or without coloured collar patches, trousers and puttees, and the M1916 version of the German M1916 helmet with typically prominent side lugs; some men are wearing the wider Slovene M1918 version. Note the double canvas shoulder bags for grenades, the assault daggers, and the clubs and maces favoured by assault troops for hand-to-hand trench fighting. Also note the gasmasks in their tin canisters, the M1895 Stützen 8mm carbines and M1907 Roth-Steyr 8mm automatic pistols. (Dusan Babac Collection)

19 November at the first battle of Monastir – the first Serbian town to be liberated – thus forcing the reinforcement of the Bulgarian 2nd Army by the Ottoman 20th Corps.

The front now settled down into a stalemate which prompted the French Prime Minister, Georges 'Tiger' Clemenceau, unfairly to label the *Armée de l'Orient* 'the Gardeners of Salonika'. The year 1917 saw minimal local gains: the British Salonika Army failed to dislodge the Bulgarian 1st Army at the battle of Lake Doiran (24-25 April and 8-9 May 1917); while in the Crna Sector, during the spring offensive, the Bulgarian 1st Army successfully resisted the Russian 2nd Brigade and Serbian 2nd Army at the second battle of Monastir (9-14 May 1917). The German 11th Army also repelled the 2nd and 3rd Divisional Groups in the Ochrid and Monastir Sectors at the battle of Lake Prespa (9-17 May 1917). The *de facto* abdication of the neutralist Greek King Constantine on 12 June 1917, and Greece's declaration of war on the Central Powers on 25 June encouraged the *Armée de l'Orient* to plan for victory. However, Greek political instability, a malaria epidemic in the British units, the growing unreliability of Russian and French troops, and a lack of firm Allied commitment to the Salonika Front delayed the final offensive. The only clear victory was the capture on 7 September 1917 of Pogradec in the Ochrid Sector from the Austro-Hungarian 19th Corps by the 3rd Divisional Group. This led to the replacement of Gen. Sarrail, the commander of the *Armée de l'Orient*, on 22 December 1917, and all Allied forces in Greece were placed under his successor, Gen. Guillaumat.

Meanwhile, on 30 May 1918 Greek divisions of the 1st Divisional Group captured the Skrá di Legen ridge, on the left bank of the Vardar in the Struma Sector, from the Bulgarian 1st Army. This galvanised Greek support for the Entente. Meanwhile, the Italian 16th Corps and the 3rd Divisional Group advanced into Central Albania in early July 1918, capturing Berat; but during 14-26 August the Austro-Hungarian Army Group Albania (formerly 19th Corps) counterattacked, retaking Berat and most of the lost territory.

The advance from Salonika commenced on 14 September 1918 with a 580-gun artillery barrage, the most powerful ever seen in the Balkans, in the Monastir, Crna and Struma Sectors. On 15 September the Serbian 2nd Army supported by two French divisions, and the Serbian 1st Army, launched the final offensive in the Crna Sector, reaching the Vardar River at Negotino on 21 September. The British Salonika Army and Greek 1st Corps commenced a limited advance on 16 September, taking Belasica on the 29th; the 1st Divisional Group attacked on the 22nd, taking Prilep and Üskub on the 29th. On 30 September Bulgaria concluded an armistice with the Allies, forcing the German 11th Army, supported by Austrian and new German divisions, to regroup at Nis; but on 12 October the Serbian 1st Army took the city, followed by Krusevac on the 17th and Belgrade on 1 November. The Italian 16th Corps and 3rd Divisional Group advanced into Central Albania on 2 October against minimal resistance, occupying Durrës on 14 October, Tirana on the 15th, Shkodër on the 31st, and reaching Bar in Montenegro on 3 November, where they met the Serbian 2nd Army, which had occupied Kosovo and Montenegro.

A Serbian infantry corporal wearing the M1908 grey-green field uniform, 1914; cf Plate B2. Note the fine example of the *sajkaca* field cap and his baggy trousers cut tight below the knee. The low-shaft marching boots gave way to traditional *opanci* footwear in 1915. He wears standard M1895 German ammunition-pouches with no supporting straps and carries a German M1899 Mauser 7mm bolt-action rifle. (Dusan Babac Collection)

Some French forces occupied Bulgaria and entered Rumania in early November, while others advanced through Greek and Bulgarian Thrace, reaching the Turkish border on 30 October. On that day the Ottoman Empire concluded an armistice, followed by Austro-Hungary on 4 November and Germany on the 11th, thereby ending the Great War.

The Rumanian campaign

On 27 August 1916 Rumania declared war on Austro-Hungary in order to annex Hungarian Transylvania, defended by the Austro-Hungarian 1st Army. On 28 August the Rumanian Northern (later 4th) Army in Moldavia crossed into Eastern Transylvania and the 1st and 2nd Armies in Wallachia entered Southern Transylvania, occupying Kronstadt (now Brasov) and Hermannstadt (Sibiu). Meanwhile, the Rumanian 3rd Army and Russian 47th Corps (from 7 September the Russo-Rumanian Dobrudja Army), combined on 15 September as the Southern Army Group, defended Southern Wallachia from the Mackensen Army Group, comprising the Bulgarian 3rd Army, German 52nd Corps and Ottoman 15th Corps. The Bulgarian-Ottoman Danube Army advanced northwards into Dobrudja on 1 September 1916, taking Constanta on 22 October, while the rest of Mackensen's force resisted the Southern Army Group's advance across the Danube at Flaminda on 1 October, before counterattacking on 23 November and advancing towards Bucharest. This halted the Rumanian offensive in Transylvania; and the Transylvanian garrison – Archduke Josef's Army Group (1st and 7th Armies, German 9th Army) – now counterattacked.

As the Austro-Hungarian 7th Army blocked the Russian 4th and 9th Armies, the Austro-Hungarian 1st and German 9th Armies retook Hermannstadt on 26 September. The German 9th Army then broke through the Rumanian 1st Army at the Targû-Jiu Gorge (23 October-18 November 1916) into Wallachia, reoccupying Kronstadt on 7 October, smashing a determined defence by the Rumanian 2nd Army of the Oituz Pass (11 October-15 November 1916), and advancing into Southern Moldavia. The Rumanian counterattack on the River Arges failed on 5 December, and Bucharest fell the next day, although the government had already transferred to Iasi in Eastern Moldavia (North-Eastern Rumania). By 31 December 1916 the Rumanian 1st, 2nd and 4th Armies and Russian 4th, 6th and 9th Armies were defending Eastern Moldavia on the Seret River Line.

By May 1917 the Allied military mission had reorganised Rumanian forces into the 1st and 2nd Armies. With vital Russian support, they promptly took the offensive, winning three important battles against Austro-German forces in Moldavia in summer 1917. At Marasti (22 July–1 August) in Southern Moldavia the Rumanian 2nd and Russian 4th Armies defeated the Austro-Hungarian 1st Army. The Rumanian 1st and Russian 4th Armies successfully resisted the German 9th Army's determined counteroffensive at Marasesti during 6 August-3 September. Finally, during 8-22 August, the Rumanian 2nd and

Subaltern officers of a Serbian field artillery battery in March 1915 in Arandjelovac, Central Serbia, standing in front of Serbian fast-loading M1907 Schneider-Cannet 7.6cm field-guns. The middle officer wears a soft M1908 officer's peaked service cap and a woollen surcoat without collar patches and shoulder boards over his field tunic. The other two officers have stiffened field caps and M1908 greatcoats with branch-colour spearhead collar patches and subaltern officers' grey-green lapels. Cf Plate B1. (Dusan Babac Collection)

A Serbian third line infantry company in 1914 wearing a mixture of M1896 dark blue and M1908 grey-green field uniform. The reserve officer commanding (5th left, front row) wears the M1908 officers' peakless field cap and M1896 greatcoat, and carries an obsolete Russian M1881 infantry sabre. He is flanked by two reserve sergeants *(narednik)*, each wearing an M1896 field cap and M1908 greatcoat and carrying the M1881 sabre as befitting their rank. Most of the remaining soldiers wear the traditional *subara* fur cap, peasants' clothes and *opanci* footwear, and carry obsolete M1870 Berdan M2 10.67mm bolt-action rifles. (Serbian National Library)

Russian 9th Armies halted the Austro-Hungarian 1st Army's counter offensive at Oituz.

Dismayed at the withdrawal of Bolshevik Russia from the war, Rumania ceased hostilities on 6 December 1917. On 7 May 1918, under the Treaty of Bucharest, she ceded the Carpathian passes to Austro-Hungary and Dobrudja to Bulgaria, but was able to annex ex-Russian Bessarabia. German and Austro-Hungarian military governments operated in occupied Wallachia from November 1916. On 10 November 1918 Rumania belatedly re-entered the war in time to joined the advance of the *Armée de l'Orient* through the Western Balkans.

THE AUSTRO-HUNGARIAN ARMY ON THE BALKAN FRONT

The Austro-Hungarian Army was a uniquely complex institution, containing multinational units drawn from 11 main nationalities – Austro-Germans, Hungarians, Italians, Rumanians, Czechs, Slovaks, Poles, Ruthenians (Ukrainians), Slovenes, Serbs and Croats – grouped into five military organizations.

The three 'first line' forces (men aged 18-33) comprised: the infantry and cavalry divisions of the Austro-Hungarian Imperial and Royal Common Army (*Kaiserliches und Königliches Gemeinsames Heer*); the infantry (*Landwehr*, redesignated 1 May 1917 'rifle' – *Schützen*) divisions of the Austrian Imperial Royal Defence Force (*Kaiserliche Königliche Landwehr)*; and infantry (*Honvédség*) and cavalry (*Huszar*) divisions of the Royal Hungarian Defence Force (*Magyar királyi Honvédség*). The Austrian Imperial Royal Territorial Army (*Kaiserlicher Königlicher Landsturm)* and the Royal Hungarian Territorial Army (*Magyar királyi Népfelkelo*) comprised 'second line' static home defence units for men aged 34-55. The language of command of Common Army and Austrian forces was German, and for Hungarian forces it was Hungarian. Some 1,800,000

Serbian infantry leave their trenches during operations in 1914 to attack Austro-Hungarian lines. The soldiers are wearing standard M1908 uniforms with *opanci* shoes and German M1895 brown leather equipment, with shoulder belts worn crossed in the Serbian style. (Dusan Babac Collection)

men were mobilised by August 1914, rising to 3,194,000 in May 1918. The Army Air Corps (*Luftschiffer- und Fliegertruppe*), part of the Common Army, and the Naval Air Corps (*Seefliegerkorps*), operated in the Western Balkans.

Balkan Slavs were the largest national component of the Austro-Hungarian forces in August 1914, with 563,400 (31.3 per cent) Serbs and Croats (including Bosnians), and 50,400 (2.8 per cent) Slovenes. Of the 16 Austro-Hungarian Corps Districts, four covered Balkan territories and recruited seven divisions: 13th Croatia-Slavonia District (7, 36 Inf. Divs.); 15th Bosnia-Herzegovina District (1, 18 Inf. Divs.); 16th Dalmatia District (4-5 Mountain Brigades); 3rd Southern Austria – Slovenia District (6, 28 Inf., 22 Rifle Divs.). The 7th *Honvédség* Croatia-Slavonia District was designated the Slavonian Defence Force (*Slavonsko Domobranstvo*) with Croatian as the language of command, its 42nd Division designated the 'Devil's Division' (*Vrazja divizija*).

Five of these divisions (1, 7, 18, 36, 42) fought in Serbia in 1914, but thereafter, with the exception of 7th Infantry Division in Rumania, served only on the Italian Front, for fear of Serb and Croat desertions. However, the trusted Bosnia-Herzegovinan units served in 37 divisions, usually on the Italian Front, but also in Serbia and Albania (18, 47, 53, 57, 59, 62-63, 81 and Eastern Corps), and Rumania (71-73).

An army group co-ordinated armies or corps, an army comprising between two and four corps or ad hoc 'forces' (*Gruppen*), each controlling between one and three divisions. Five armies with 42 divisions served in the Balkans.

Eighteen (including five Balkan) divisions fought on the Serbian Front in 1914: 5th Army with 8th Corps (9 Inf., 21 *Landwehr* Divs.) and 13th Corps (36 Inf., 42 *Domobranstvo* Divs.); 6th Army with 15th Corps (1, 48 Inf. Divs.) and 16th Corps (18 Inf. Div.); five Balkan Army HQ divisions (7, 47 Inf., 23, 40 *Honvédség* Divs.); and until August 1914 2nd Army with 4th Corps (31-32 Inf., 5 *Huszar* Divs.), 7th Corps (17, 34 Inf. Divs.) and 9th Corps (29 Inf. Division).

Nine divisions fought in 1915, in 3rd Army's 11th Corps (30, 53 Inf. Divs.) and 14th Corps (8, 13 Inf., 44 *Landwehr* Divs.), and the independent 57th, 59th, 62nd and 63rd Infantry Divisions. The Albanian garrison comprised 19th Corps (47, 81 Inf. Divs., 220 *Landsturm* Bde.), in August 1918 redesignated Army Group Albania. Bosnia-Herzegovina and Dalmatia Command had the 45th *Landwehr* Division, the Montenegro Occupation Force six battalions and the Serbian five. In September 1918 11th Corps (9, 30 Inf. Divs.) reinforced German

11th Army in Macedonia; and the four-battalion Eastern Corps *(Orientkorps)*, intended for Palestine, helped defend Albania.

In August 1916 Hungarian Transylvania was garrisoned by 1st Army (61, 71 Inf. Divs., 143-5 Inf. Bdes., 16, 19 Inf., 1 Cav. *Népfelkelo* Bde., later 10, 11 Bavarian Infantry Divisions). Three divisions (51 *Honvédség*, 73 Inf., 1 Cav.) and three *Népfelkelo* brigades (2, 8, 10) several in German 9th Army, both these armies forming part of Archduke Josef's Army Group. Fourteen Austro-Hungarian and six German units formed 1st Army in June 1917: Gerok Force with Ruiz Force (1 Cav., 37 Inf., 218 German Inf. Divs.), and 8th Corps (70, 71 Inf., 8 Cav. Div., 8 Mount. Bde., 142 Inf. Bde.); Liposchak Force (7 Inf., 8 Bavarian Inf., 10 Cav. Divs., 16 Mount. Bde.); 6th Corps (39 *Honvédség*, 117, 225 German Inf. Divs.); and 21st Corps (31, 37, 72 Inf. Divs., 3 German Cavalry Division).

SERBIA

The Serbs revolted against Ottoman rule in February 1804. By July 1914 the Kingdom of Serbia, under King Petar I Karageorgevic, comprised about 4,700,000 Serbs with Macedonian and Albanian minorities, covering 38,200 square miles of present-day Serbia (excluding Vojvodina), Kosovo and most of Macedonia, annexed as 'South Serbia' on 30 May 1913 after the First Balkan War.

The Serbian Army *(Srpska Vojska)* deployed units of the 'first line' (men aged 21-31) and 'second line' (men aged 32-37) of the National Army *(Narodna Vojska)* in the field army, and 'third line' (men aged 38-45) and Territorial – *Poskania Odbrana* (men aged 18-20 and 46-50) – units on garrison and lines-of-communication duties. Pre-1913 Serbia was divided into five corps-status Military Districts – 1st Morava, 2nd Drina, 3rd Dunav (Danube), 4th Sumadija and 5th Timok – each named after local rivers, and recruiting one first line *(posiv*, in German *Ban)* infantry division, three third line infantry regiments, one company-status third line cavalry squadron, and a number of territorial infantry battalions and cavalry squadrons. There were also traditional irregular Chetnik guerrilla detachments *(Odredi)* and companies. Five more districts – 6th Ibar, 7th Kosovo, 8th Vardar, 9th Bregalnica and 10th Monastir – were established in August 1913 in South Serbia but by July 1914 were only able to recruit the 'Composite' *(Kombinovna)* infantry division, followed in 1915 by the Vardar and embryonic Bregalnica Divisions. The Cavalry Division recruited nationally. There was also a Royal Guard Regiment (two mounted squadrons – 416 men), Frontier Troops, an Army Air Corps (formed 24 December 1912) and five paramilitary Gendarmerie (rural police) battalions.

A splendidly moustachioed and bearded Serbian cavalryman in Salonika acting as ensign of a supernumerary cavalry regiment. He wears the French M1915 'horizon blue' field uniform with infantry puttees and ankle boots and a khaki-painted M1915 Adrian helmet with Serbian badge. He carries the M1895 Other Ranks' cavalry sabre, a pistol, waterbottle and canvas bag. The flags of the supernumerary regiments had a painted (M1911 flags were embroidered) Serbian eagle with the motto 'For King and Fatherland/with Faith in God'. St.Andrew and campaign streamers were on the reverse. (Dusan Babac Collection)

Two Serbian infantrymen in Salonika in 1918, wearing – unusually – the US Army M1902 khaki field tunic, breeches and puttees, with Serbian M1908 field caps. They have French brown leather M1916 equipment and carry 8mm Lebel 86/93 bolt-action rifles with open breeches. The Serbian and SHS armies continued to wear Serbian, British, French, Russian and United States uniforms and equipment until new regulations were issued on 2 March 1922. (Dusan Babac Collection)

A first line infantry division, with 430 officers and 19,000 other ranks, comprised four infantry regiments (four battalions per 4,112-man regiment, each 1,112-man battalion with one machine gun and four infantry companies); a cavalry regiment (four 130-man squadrons); a field artillery regiment (three battalions, each with three four-gun batteries); divisional services – two engineer companies, bridging and signals sections; supply and ammunition columns; a medical company and four field ambulances. A second line division had 15,000 men in three infantry regiments; a cavalry regiment (two squadrons); a field artillery battalion; and reduced divisional services. The Cavalry Division, with 60 officers and 11,900 other ranks, had two brigades, each with two 850-man cavalry regiments (one machine gun and four mounted 210-man squadrons per regiment); one horse-artillery battalion (two four-gun batteries); divisional services, mounted signals section and ammunition column.

The C-in-C was Crown Prince Aleksandar, with Field Marshal Radomir Putnik, the most gifted general in the Balkans during the Great War, as Chief of the General Staff and Maj. Gen. Zivojin Misic as his deputy. By 30 July 1914 Putnik had mobilised about 420,500 men in five armies led by generals who had been Putnik's able pupils at the Serbian Military Academy. These were 1st Army under Maj. Gen. Petar Bojovic, later Field Marshal Misic; 2nd Army under Maj. Gen. Stepan Stepanovic; 3rd Army under Maj. Gen. Pavle Jurisic-Sturm; Uzice Army under Maj. Gen. Milos Bozanovic; New Military Districts Army under Maj. Gen. Bojovic; and four divisional-status detachments. The Serbian Army, battle-hardened in the two Balkan Wars, repelled three Austro-Hungarian invasions in 1914. However, in November 1915, weakened by the diversion of the 20,000-man Albanian Detachment (Maj. Gen. Dragutin Milutinovic) to Albania, the 400,000-man main force conducted the 'Albanian Retreat' to Corfu, with soldiers doggedly carrying the ailing Putnik in a sedan-chair across the icy Prokletije mountains.

From November 1915 to September 1918 Eastern Serbia was annexed by Bulgaria, and 'Old Serbia' (Serbia less Kosovo and Macedonia) was under Austro-Hungarian military government, with the rest of Serbia under joint Central Powers military occupation. About 3,500 Austro-Hungarian Gendarmerie and Military Police opposed a determined resistance campaign by Serbian Chetnik guerrillas, while Bulgarian troops put down the Toplica Uprising (February-March 1917) in Eastern Serbia.

Some 145,000 Serbian troops evacuated to Corfu where, by 15 April 1916, the Serbian Army, under Field Marshal Misic with Maj. Gen. Bojovic as Chief of Staff, re-formed into three armies, each grouping two reconstituted infantry divisions – 1st Army (Colonel Milos Vasic), 2nd Army (Field Marshal Stepanovic) and 3rd Army (Maj. Gen.

1 Army:- (1914) Cavalry, Danube/2, Morava/2, Timok/1, Timok/2, Branicevo Det; (1915) Danube/2. Drina/2; (1916) Morava, Vardar; (1917) Danube, Drina, Morava, Cavalry.

2 Army:- (1914) Composite, Danube/1, Morava/1, Sumadija/1; (1915) Timok/1, Sumadija/2; (1916) Sumadija, Timok; (1917) Sumadija, Timok, Yugoslav.

3 Army:- (1914) Drina/1, Drina/2, Belgrade Det, Frontier Det; (1915) Danube/1, Drina/1, Belgrade Det; (1916) Danube, Drina.

New Military Districts (South Serbian) Army:- (1914) 7-19 Sup.Rgt; 13 art bat; (1915) Morava/1, Morava/2, Vardar.

Timok Army:- (1915) Cavalry, Composite, 6 inf.rgts.

Uzice Army:- (1914) Sumadija/2, Uzice Brigade.

1st Moravska Military District (Nis) – South-Central Serbia
Morava Div/1:-1-3,16 Inf.Rgt/1; Morava/1 Cav.Rgt; Morava/1 Art.Rgt; Morava/1 services. Morava Div/2:- 1-3 Inf.Rgt/2; Morava/2 Cav.Rgt; Morava/2 Art.Bn; Morava/2 services. Uzice Brigade (1-3 Inf.Rgt/3); Morava/3 Cav.Sqn.

2nd Drinska Military District (Valjevo) – Western Serbia
Drina Div/1:- 4 (3 Sup.)-6,17 Inf.Rgt/1; Drina/1 Cav.Rgt; Drina/1 Art.Rgt; Drina/1 services. Drina Div/2:- 4-6 Inf.Rgt/2; Drina/2 Cav.Rgt; Drina/2 Art.Bn; Drina/2 services. 4-6 Inf.Rgt/3; Drina/3 Cav.Sqn.

3rd Dunavska Military District (Belgrade) – Northern Serbia
Danube Div/1:-7,8,18,9 (4 Sup.) Inf.Rgt/1;Danube/1 Cav.Rgt; Danube/1 Art.Rgt;Danube/1 serv. Danube Div/2:- 7-9 Inf.Rgt/2; Danube/2 Cav.Rgt; Danube/2 Art.Bn; Danube/2 services. 7-9 Inf.Rgt/3; Danube/3 Cav.Sqn.

4th Sumadijska Military District (Kragujevac) – Central Serbia
Sumadija Div/1:-10-12,19 Inf.Rgt/1; Sumadija/1 Cav.Rgt; Sumadija/1 Art.Rgt; Sumadija/1 serv. Sumadija Div/2:-10-12 Inf.Rgt/2; Sumadija/2 Cav.Rgt; Sumadija/2 Art.Bn; Sumadija/2 services. 10-12 Inf.Rgt/3; Sumadija/3 Cav.Sqn.

5th Timocka Military District (Zajecar) – Eastern Serbia
Timok Div/1:- 13-15,20 Inf.Rgt/1; Timok/1 Cav.Rgt; Timok/1 Art.Rgt; Timok/1 services. Timok Div/2:- 13-15 Inf.Rgt/2; Timok/2 Cav.Rgt; Timok/2 Art.Bn; Timok/2 services. 13-15 Inf.Rgt/3; Timok/3 Cav.Sqn.

Southern Serbia Military Districts:- 6th Ibar (Novi Pazar); 7th Kosovo (Pristina); 8th Vardar (Skopje/Uskub); 9th Bregalnica (Stip); 10th Monastir (Bitola/Monastir).
Composite (Kombinovana) Div:- 1,2,5, 6 Sup.Rgt; Comp. Cav.Rgt; Comp. Art Rgt; Comp.services. Vardar Div:-21-24 Inf.Rgt/1;Vardar Inf. Rgt/3 Vardar Cav.Rgt;Vardar Art.Rgt;Vardar serv. Bregalnicka Division:- various Bregalnica Military District troops.

Cavalry Div:- 1st Brigade (1,3 Cav.Rgt); 2nd Brigade (2,4 Cav.Rgt); Horse Art.Rgt, Div.services
Air Corps:- N87, F98, N387, F382 (later AR521), F398, N523 Squadrons.

Belgrade Detachment:- (1914) 8/3,11/3,15/3 Inf.Rgt, 9 art.bat. (1915) Timok/2, Sumadija/1.
Branicevo Detachment:- Danube/2.
Frontier Detachment:- 4-9/3, 13/3 Inf.Rgt, 13 art bat.
Obrenovac Detachment:- 10/3,14/3,19/3 Inf.Rgt, 5 art bat.

1st Div. Serbian Volunteer Corps:- 1-3 Inf.Rgt; Cav.Rgt; Art.Rgt; services
2nd Div. Serbian Volunteer Corps:- 4-6 Inf.Rgt; Cav.Rgt; Art.Rgt; services

---

Jurisic-Sturm), the last army disbanding on 28 March 1917. Each 20,000-man division comprised a first line, second line and third line infantry regiment each with three battalions of three companies and a machine gun section. There was also a 150-man cavalry squadron; a field artillery regiment (three two-battery battalions); and divisional services – two engineer companies and engineer park; bakery and artificer companies; two supply columns; a medical company and three field ambulances. The 12,000-man Vardar Division absorbed the Composite Division, and the Cavalry Division was reformed. In late June 1916 the 18,000-strong 1st Serbian Volunteer Division was created from Balkan prisoners-of-war in Russia and fought in the Russo-Rumanian Dobrudja Army. In September 1916 a second was formed and both divisions were grouped into the Serbian Volunteer Corps *(Srpski Dobrovoljacki Korpus)* in Odessa, under Maj. Gen. Mihailo Zivkovic. In 1917 this 28,000-man force joined the Serbian Army on the Salonika Front as the Yugoslav Division. The Serbian Army spearheaded the advance into Macedonia in September 1918 which helped eliminate the Bulgarian and Austro-Hungarian armies from the war. The heroic achievements of the Serbian Army during the Great War earned it a central place in Serbian history and also the admiration of the Entente, who granted Serbia political leadership of the SHS Kingdom, formed on 1 December 1918.

A Montenegrin Army captain in M1910 full-dress uniform with peaked service cap (with captain's cap-badge) and plain collar. General officers had gold epaulettes with thick bullion-fringes and 0, 3, 2 and 1 silver five-pointed stars; field officers thin fringes and 1 star, subaltern officers no fringes and 3-1 stars. Note the stars positioned two-over-one in the Serbian manner, rather than the regulation one-over-two, demonstrating the officer's pro-Serbian loyalties. He wears the Montenegrin M1896 officer's sword, a copy of the Russian M1881, on a full dress silver braid-faced belt, and the 1910 Medal commemorating the elevation of the Principality of Montenegro to a Kingdom. (Dusan Babac Collection)

MONTENEGRO

Ethnic Serbs inhabiting Mount Lovcen – the 'Black Mountain' – had preserved their independence from Ottoman occupation since 1485; and in 1914 Montenegro, under King Nikola I, was the oldest and smallest independent Balkan state, comprising about 400,000 Serbs with an Albanian minority, and covered 5,800 square miles.

The Montenegrin Army (*Crnagorska Vojska*), traditionally a wartime clan militia, was modernised in 1906. The first line field army comprised recruits aged 18-19 completing 12 months', military service and trained soldiers aged 20-53, with men aged 53-62 in the second line reserve army (*Narodna Vojska*). In 1914 Montenegro was divided into six Divisional Military Districts. Each division had 4,000-6,000 men divided into two or three infantry brigades, heavy and field artillery batteries consisting of 100 men each, and a supply company. A brigade (about 2,000 men) had between five and ten infantry battalions (each 400-500 strong) in about four or five clan based companies, each with five platoons; a 100-man mountain artillery battery; 40-man reconnaissance and 36-man machine gun companies; a 30-man medical and a 40-man engineer platoon (including four-man signals section), all numbered 1-16 with the brigade number. The Montenegrin Red Cross constituted the medical corps. There was also a 100-man Royal Bodyguard and a Gendarmerie (*Zandarmerija*), but no cavalry, air corps or navy.

The C-in-C was King Nikola I, with Inspector-General Crown Prince Danilo the commander. However, in July 1914 King Nikola, influenced by pro-Serb political advisers, signed a defensive pact with Serbia delegating operational command of the Montenegrin Army from 23 August 1914 to Serbian Maj. Gen. Bozidar Jankovic as Chief of Staff,

Personnel of a Montenegrin machine gun company wearing M1910 field uniforms and operating the German M1912 Maxim heavy machine gun. The subaltern officer (right) wears typical field uniform with a pillbox field cap with rank cap badge and no shoulder boards, and non-regulation *opanci* shoes, as defined by Uniform Regulations. He carries officers' binoculars and the Russian M1881 officers' sword. (Military Museum, Belgrade)

leading about 200 seconded Serbian personnel. On 28 July 1914 Jankovic mobilised 35,000 men in six divisions (16 brigades, about 79 infantry battalions), with 61 battalions deployed in four division-sized detachments. Three detachments (29,000 men) confronted Austro-Hungarian forces – Lovcen (Maj. Gen. Mitar Martinovic) with 18 battalions in Southern Montenegro; Herzegovinian (Maj. Gen. Janko Vukotic, later Maj. Gen. Martinovic) with 20 battalions in Western Montenegro; and Pljevlja (Brigadier Luka Gojnic) with ten battalions in Sanjak. These forces repelled the Austro-Hungarian 16th Corps (6th Army) in 1914. Meanwhile, 6,000 men (13 battalions) in the Old Serbia Detachment (Brig. Radomir Vesovic) guarded the Albanian frontier on Gen. Jankovic's orders.

On 20 May 1915 the Montenegrin Army was expanded to 48,244 men in 19 brigades (86 $\frac{1}{2}$ infantry battalions), with 21,856 deployed in the Lovcen (Brig. Gojnic), Herzegovinian (Duke Djuro Petrovic) and Old

A fine study of a Montenegrin sergeant in regulation M1910 khaki service uniform, wearing his white metal rank cap badge and the Other Ranks' tunic with the distinctive khaki cloth sash, and the 1910 Commemoration Medal. Note that the regulation NCOs' branch-colour shoulder strap loops were never in fact worn. See Plate D2. (Miladin Markovic Collection)

Army of the Kingdom of Montenegro

28 July 1914–20 May 1915
Lovcen Detachment (Lovcenski Odred) – Southern Montenegro. About 8,000 men.
1 Cetinjska Division (Cetinje) – 1 Heavy Art.Bty; 1 Field Art.Bty, 1 Supply Company. 1 Katunska Brig:- Cetinjski, Cucki, Cevsko-Bijelicko, Pjesivacki, Komansko-Zagaracki, Njegusko-Ceklicki Bns 2 Rijecko-Ljesanska Brigade:- Ljubotinski, Gornjo-Ceklinski, Donji-Ceklinski, Ljesanski Bns. 3 Primorska-Crmnicka Brigade:- Gornjo Crmnicki, Donjo Crmnicki, Seljacko, Barski, Ulcinjski, Krajinski, Mrkojevicki Bns.
2 Podgoricka Division (Podgorica) – 2 Heavy Art.Bty; 2 Field Art. Bty, 1 Supply Company. 4 Zetska Brigade:- Donjo-Kucko, Zetski, Gornjo-Kucko, Bratonozicki, Podgoricki, Zatrijevacki Bns. 5 Spuzka Brigade:- Piperski, Ljeskopolski, Spuzki Bns. 6 Brdska Brigade:- Brajovicko-Martinicki, Pavkovicki, Petrusinski, Vraze Grmski Bns.
Herzegovinian Detachment (Hercegovacki Odred) – Western Montenegro. About 15,000 men.
3 Niksicka Division (Niksic) – 3 Heavy Art.Bty; 3 Field Art.Bty, 3 Supply Company. 7 Niksicka Brigade:- Trebjeski, Niksicki, Lukovski, Zupski, Goljiski Bns. 8 Vucedolska Brigade:- Grahovksi, Rudinski-Trepacki, Oputno-Rudinski, Banjanski Bns. 9 Durmitorska Brigade:- Zupa-Pivska, Drobnjacki, Uskocki, Planine Pivski, Jezero Bns.
4 Kolasinska Division (Kolasin) – 4 Heavy Art.Bty; 4 Field Art.Bty, 4 Supply Company. 10 Kolasinska Brigade:- Donjo Moracki, Lipovski, Rovacki, Kolasinski, Gornjo Moracki, Poljski Bns. 11 Vasojevicka Brigade:- Ljevorecki, Kraljski, Andrijevicki, Polimski, Trepacki-Sekularski, Veljicki Bns.

Pljevlja Detachment (Pljevljski Odred) – Northern Montenegro (Sanjak). About 6,000 men.
5 Pljevljska Division (Pljevlja) – 5 Heavy Art.Bty; 5 Field Art.Bty, 5 Supply Company. 12 Pljevljska Brigade:- 5 ? battalions. 13 Bjelopoljska Brigade:- 5 ? battalions.
Old Serbia Detachment (Starosrbijanski Odred) – South-Eastern Montenegro. About 6,000 men.
6 Pecka Division (Pec) – 6 Heavy Art.Bty; 6 Field Art.Bty, 6 Supply Company. 14 Pecka Brigade:- 3 ? battalions. 15 Rozajska Brigade:- 3 ? battalions. 16 Plavo-Gusinjska Brigade:- 2 ? battalions.

20 May 1915–25 January 1916
Lovcen Detachment (Lovcenski Odred) – 6,902 men, 42 artillery pieces, 11 machine guns. Katunska, Primorska-Crmnicka, Zetska Brigades.
Herzegovinian Detachment (Hercegovacki Odred) – 10,149 men, 19 artillery-pieces, 11 machine guns. Bjelopavlicka,[1] Niksicka, Spuzka, Vucedolska Brigades.
Old Serbia Detachment (Starosrbijanski Odred) – 4,805 men, 20 artillery-pieces, 10 machine guns. Donjo Vasojevicka,[1] Gornjo Vasojevicka,1 Pecka Brigades; Decani, Djakovica, Pec, Tuzi detachments.
Sandzacka Vojska (Sanjak Army) – 26,388 men, 54 artillery pieces, 39 machine guns. 1 Sanjak Division:- Decanska,[1] Bjelopoljska Brigades. 2 Sanjak Division:- Lovcenska,[1] Pljevaljska, Vasojevicka Brigades. Drinska Division:- Durmitorska, Kolasinska, Kucko Bratonoska,[1] Rijecko-Ljesanska Brigades.

[1] Brigade newly formed in September 1915.

15

Major-General Nikola Zhekov, the pro-German Commander of the Bulgarian Armed Forces during the Great War, photographed in 1915. Zhekov is wearing the M1908 superior quality officers' grey-green service tunic with red branch-colour collar and pointed cuff piping, and gold Russia-braid shoulder boards piped red with one silver rank pip. Amongst his medals are the Military Order for Bravery in War, Ottoman War Medal breast star, 1914 Iron Cross 1st Class breast medal and 2nd Class medal on a button-ribbon. (Nigel Thomas Collection)

Serbia (Brig. Vesovic) Detachments, and 26,388 (55 per cent of the forces) in the Sanjak Army (Maj. Gen. Vukotic), ensuring contact with Serbian forces. In June 1915, however, King Nikola marginalised Jankovic by ordering 'Old Serbia' to occupy Shkodër in Northern Albania, prompting Jankovic's resignation and replacement by the Serbian Col. Petar Pesic. In October 1915 King Nikola refused to allow outnumbered Montenegrin forces to retreat with the Serb main force. The Sanjak Army covered the Serbian retreat by engaging Austro-Hungarian forces at Kalinovik, Klobuk and Foca in Eastern Herzegovina, winning an important victory at Mojkovac in Sanjak during 6-7 January 1916 with 6,000 losses. Nevertheless, on 25 December 1915 Austro-Hungarian forces entered Montenegro and took Mount Lovcen, defended by 15,000 Montenegrins, on 10 January 1916; and on 25 January the Montenegrin Army surrendered.

Austro-Hungarian Gendarmerie and Military Police fought a savage campaign against Chetnik guerrillas under Defence Minister Brig. Vesovic until 31 December 1917. The 1st-3rd Battalions of Montenegrin emigrés were formed by Petar Lekic at Gaeta, near Naples, but did not see action. King Nikola settled in exile in Bordeaux, but his attempts in December 1915 to negotiate a separate peace with Austro-Hungary had destroyed his credibility with the Entente. On 23 October 1918 Serbian 2nd Army occupied Montenegro; and on 26 November 1918 the only Entente nation in the Great War to lose its independence joined the SHS Kingdom as Zeta Province. Armed opposition to the Serbian annexation, led by Col. Krsto Popovic, lasted from 7 January 1919 (the orthodox Christmas) until 1926.

ALBANIA

Albania declared independence on 28 November 1912, its territory covering about 11,500 square miles with about 800,000 Albanians, and a Greek minority in the south in Northern Epirus. From the first, however, it was torn by internal political intrigues and international hostility. An Albanian National Army *(Ushtria Kombëtar Shqiptar)* was formed in May 1913 under Col. Ali Shefqeti, but on 22 January 1914 the pro-Serbian Defence Minister, Esad Pashë Toptani, commanding the 4,000-strong Gendarmerie *(Xhandarmëria)*, organised in four detachments (1st-4th), staged a coup. The army, well short of its planned strength of 12,000 men, refused to serve under Esad, whose gendarmes effectively controlled only Central Albania. Northern Albania was controlled by Bajram Curri with 20,000 men, many of whom were Kosovar and Macedonian refugees, backed by Austro-Hungary and the Catholic Mirditë clans; and Central Albania was under Haxhi Qerim's 'Union of Krujë'. Northern Epirus, autonomous since 17 February 1914, was occupied by the Greek Army in November (and formally annexed to Greece on 18 March 1916); and on 28 December 1914 an Italian expeditionary force occupied the Vlorë district.

On 29 May 1915 the Serbian Army occupied Northern and Central Albania to disperse Curri's insurgents and relieve Esad, besieged in Durrës. Later, in December 1915, Serbian forces retreating through the Mati Region of Central Albania were attacked by Curri but assisted by

A corporal *(Unteroffizier)* of a German infantry regiment, off duty in Pozarevac, Central Serbia, 9 October 1918. He is wearing the M1915 service and field uniform (introduced 21 September 1915). On the field-grey *Bluse* with roll-back cuffs and fly front the corporal's rank insignia is reduced to a silver or gold braid chevron on the front of the collar. He wears an M1907 field-grey Other Ranks' field cap with branch-colour cap band and crown piping, stone-grey trousers, blackened marching boots, M1909 belt with Contingent badge, M1898 bayonet with junior NCOs' and men's silver and company colour bayonet knot. (Dusan Babac Collection)

Esad's gendarmes. Italian forces covered the Serb embarkation at Durrës before evacuating to Italy on 24 February 1916 with Esad and several hundred gendarmes. On 20 March 1916 the Italian Special Albania Corps (its title since December 1915) with three infantry divisions – 38th (*Savona, Puglie* Bdes.); 43rd (*Arno, Marche* Bdes.) and 44th (*Taranto, Verona* Bdes.) – was redesignated 16th Corps and, on 20 June 1916, the 'Albanian Occupation Troops' after 43rd and 44th Divisions had repatriated, recruiting Albanian irregulars. On 23 August 1916 the Italians, with Allied permission, occupied Northern Epirus, forcing the neutralist Greek Army to withdraw.

From January 1916 the Austro-Hungarian 19th Corps occupied Northern and Central Albania, deploying Curri's tribal irregulars and establishing an Albanian Legion (*Albanische Legion*) with Austro-Hungarian officers and senior NCOs, comprising nine infantry battalions, each with four companies 150-175 strong. Austro-Hungarian Gendarmerie and Military Police, their ranks swelled by Albanian recruits, exercised a relatively benign occupation regime.

Esad reached Salonika in late August 1916 with 800 Albanian gendarmes; and in December 1916 Gen. Sarrail set him up in the 'Republic of Korçë' in the Ochrid Sector of Northern Epirus controlled by the *Armée de l'Orient*'s 3rd Divisional Group. Esad's gendarmes fought well in a raid in September 1917, and were allocated the Allied front between Pogradec and the Shkumbi River. The secret Allied Treaty of London of 26 April 1915 prescribed the partition of Albania – technically an Entente state – and on 3 June 1917 the Italian Gen. Ferrero proclaimed an Italian protectorate in Central and Southern Albania (Northern Albania was allocated to Serbia and Montenegro). On 12 October 1918 the French disbanded Esad's gendarmes and on 10 December dissolved the Korçë Republic.

On 19 June 1917 the Italian Albanian Occupation Troops were redesignated 16th Corps and by September comprised three infantry divisions – 13th (*Barletta, Palermo* Bdes.); 36th (*Puglie, Tanaro* Bdes.) and 38th (*Savona, Verona* Bdes.) and 9th Cavalry Brigade. By 31 October 1918 Italian and French forces had expelled the Austro-Hungarian Army from Albania, but then 3,000 Albanian peasants under Bajram Curri attacked the Italians, forcing them to withdraw from Albania by 2 September 1920.

THE GERMAN ARMY ON THE BALKAN FRONT

The German Army *(Reichsheer)*, 3,823,000 strong in July 1914, grouped the Prussian, Bavarian, Saxon and Württemberg Contingents under Prussian leadership, although Bavarian units were numbered separately. The Air Corps *(Luftstreitkräfte)* was part of the army.

All German formations in the Balkans contained Austro-Hungarian (AH), Bulgarian and Ottoman units. A German army group contained two or three armies and an army comprised two or three corps, a reserve corps, a special corps *(Generalkommando z.b.V –* a corps without corps HQ troops) or ad hoc 'forces' *(Gruppen)*, named after their commander; a corps controlled between two and four divisions. From 1915 to 1918,

32 divisions served in the Balkans: 25 infantry, three reserve, one territorial *(Landwehr)* and three cavalry – a fraction of those deployed on the more critical Western and Eastern Fronts, where Germany essentially fought alone.

Only eight German divisions served in the Western Balkans. Army Group Mackensen, formed 30 September 1915 by the charismatic Prussian cavalry Field Marshal August von Mackensen, contained the German 11th Army with 3rd Corps (6 Inf., 25 Res. Div.), 4th Reserve Corps (101, 103 Inf. Div.) and 10th Reserve Corps (105, 107 Inf. Division). It served in Serbia and Macedonia until 30 July 1916, leaving 11th Army with the 101st Infantry Division to supervise Bulgarian units. In November 1916 the Hippel Division was raised with Bulgarian troops under German officers, and reorganised in January 1917 as the 302nd Infantry Division with all German personnel. On 22 April 1917 Army Group Scholtz (Lt. Gen. Scholtz) was formed to co-ordinate all forces on the Salonika Front, and the 11th Army was reinforced in October 1918 by the 217th and 210th Infantry Divisions to help resist the Allied advance from Salonika.

In contrast, 16 divisions served in the 1916 Rumanian campaign. On 15 August 1916 Army Group Mackensen reached Northern Bulgaria, its mainly Bulgarian forces supported by elements of the German 101st Infantry Division and the Hammerstein brigade-group. On 6 September 1916 more German troops arrived as 9th Army with 1st Reserve Corps (3 Cav., 89, 216 Inf. Div., from October 76 Res., 12 Bavarian Inf. Div., 8 AH Mount. Bde.), 39th Reserve Corps (48, 76 Res., 187 Inf., 51 *Honvédség* Div.), and the division-status Alpine Corps *(Alpenkorps)*. In October Schmettow Cavalry Corps (1, 3 Cav., 71 AH Inf. Div.); 'Kneussl Force' (6th Cav., 11 Bavarian Inf. Div., 144 AH Inf. Bde.) and 'Krafft Force' (Alpine Corps, 216 Inf., 73 AH Inf. Div., 2, 10 *Népfelkelo* Bde.) joined the 9th Army. In November 1916 'Kühne Force', later 54th Special Corps (41, 109, 115 Inf., 11 Bavarian Inf. Div.) and 'Staabs Force' (89 Inf., 51 *Honvédség* Div.) also joined, with 'Kosch Force', later 52nd Special Corps (217 Inf., 26 Ottoman Inf., 1, 12 Bulgarian Inf. Div., Goltz Detachment) in Dobrudja.

For the 1917 campaign Army Group Mackensen fielded 15 divisions. Its 9th Army had 1st Reserve Corps (89, 115, 212, 216 Inf., 76 Res., 12 Bavarian Inf., 13 AH Inf. Div., Alpine Corps); 18th Corps (217 Inf, 62 AH Inf. Div.) and Schaer Force (92, 109, 115 Inf. Div.); with 52nd Special Corps (Goltz Detachment, 145 AH Inf. Bde., 15, 25 Ottoman Inf. Div.) in the 3rd Bulgarian Army, and six divisions (117, 218, 225 Inf., 8 Bavarian Res., 3 Cav. Div.) in the Austro-Hungarian 1st Army. By October 1918 three more divisions (93, 226 Inf., 16 Territorial) had joined the Austro-Hungarian-German force occupying Wallachia and Western Moldavia.

Although most German divisions were not first class units they acted as the assault spearhead

Personnel of the German light infantry (Jäger) battalions (from May 1915 organised into regiments) wore M1907 uniforms of a distinctly greener cloth than standard 'field grey'. These two Prussian riflemen are wearing the M1907 field tunic (modified on 3 March 1915) with plain cuffs, and the traditional light Infantry shako with a uniform cloth cover that has an unofficial hole to show the oval Prussian cockade. They each have a single obsolete M1895 ammunition pouch, suggesting light guard duties, and carry the standard Gewehr 98 7.92mm bolt-action rifle. (Dusan Babac Collection)

and defensive backbone of the Bulgarian and Austro-Hungarian armies; but they were too few to bolster demoralised Bulgarian forces in September 1918 and prevent the powerful Allied advance from Salonika. On the Rumanian front, however, the larger German forces, allied to more Austro-Hungarian units resolutely defending national territory, dominated Rumania until November 1918, before repatriating to Germany in good order.

An Ottoman field officer (back row, middle) and subaltern officers in September 1913, wearing M1909 khaki uniforms worn during the Great War. All are wearing the service uniform black lambskin *kalpak* cap with a red cloth crown and a silver braid crown-cross, and the M1909 officers' field tunic with branch-colour collar; the field officer wears a non-standard version with external pockets. Note the German 6 x 30 standard field binoculars and the display of artillery shells. (Dusan Babac Collection)

THE OTTOMAN ARMY ON THE BALKAN FRONT

Central Powers solidarity led the Ottoman Empire to field $4\frac{1}{4}$ divisions in the Balkans to assist Bulgaria. The Rumelia Field Detachment (177th Inf. Regt.) joined the Bulgarian 4th Army in Western Thrace in September 1915, transferring to the Bulgarian 1st Army in Monastir from January 1916, while 20th Corps (26, 54 Inf. Div.) supported Bulgarian 2nd Army in the Struma Sector of the Salonika Front from early 1917. The Bulgarian 3rd Army was joined by 6th Corps (25, 26 Inf. Div.) to form the Danube Army in Rumanian Dobrudja from September to December 1916; and in January 1917 the 15th Infantry Division, having replaced the 26th, helped garrison Dobrudja and Wallachia under Army Group Mackensen. Ottoman forces withdrew following the Bulgarian Armistice of 30 September 1918.

ENTENTE FORCES IN SALONIKA

The Salonika Expeditionary Force contained contingents from the four Entente 'Great Powers' (France, Great Britain, Italy and Russia) and Serbia. The French-commanded Army of the East *(Armée de l'Orient)*, formally constituted on 12 October 1915 under Gen. Paul Sarrail, eventually comprised ten French, Italian and Russian divisions grouped into three corps-status 'Groups of Divisions', and eight Serbian divisions. On 22 December 1917 Sarrail was replaced by Gen. Marie Guillaumat, whose command expanded to include the British Salonika and Greek Armies as the Allied Armies of the East *(Armées alliées de l'Orient)*, deployed in seven sectors on South-Eastern Albanian and Greek Macedonian borders. In June 1918 Guillaumat was succeeded by Gen. Louis Franchet d'Esperey, now commanding 620,000 troops.

The **British** Salonika Army was formed on 4 November 1915 under Gen. Sir C. C. Monro. From 11 November it was commanded by Lt. Gen. Sir Bryan Mahon, and by Lt. Gen. (later Gen.) George Milne from 9 May 1916. The six infantry divisions were grouped into 12th Corps (22, 26, 60 Div.) and 16th Corps (10, 27, 28) with constant movement between corps. A 16,000-strong British infantry division in Macedonia comprised three infantry brigades (each with four, three in 1918, infantry battalions with 800 men divided into four rifle companies; a trench-mortar battery, a machine gun company and a small arms ammunition column); a divisional cyclist company (until 1917); four field artillery brigades (each with between three and six batteries) and ammunition columns; a divisional artillery ammunition column; between one and three engineer field companies; a signal company; a pioneer (labour) battalion; three heavy machine gun companies (1918); three medical field ambulances (battalions); a mobile veterinary section; an employment company; and a Service Corps supply train (four companies).

The **French** contingent, commanded by Gen. Cordonnier (from February 1917 by Gen. Grossetti, and from January 1918 by Gen. Henrys) comprised, in October 1915, five infantry divisions (57, 76, 122, 156, 158) and the Cavalry Brigade, later joined by three Colonial infantry divisions – the 17th (February 1916), 16th (December 1916) and 11th (January 1917). A French infantry division had 16,000 men in three infantry regiments each with three four-company battalions; a cavalry 'squadron' (company); a field artillery regiment with three three-battery battalions; an engineer company; a supply column and medical field ambulance. A Colonial infantry division, comprising French nationals volunteering for overseas service, retained the pre-1915 divisional organisation of four infantry regiments in two infantry brigades. The Cavalry Brigade, under Brig. Jouinot-Gambetta, had 1st and 4th *Chasseurs d'Afrique* (North African European cavalry) regiments, six Moroccan *Spahi* (North African native cavalry) squadrons and an armoured-car platoon.

The **Italian** 35th Infantry Division (Lt. Gen. Mombelli) reached Salonika on 11 August 1916. Initially it was organised as a standard Italian infantry division with two first line infantry brigades (*Cagliari*, *Sicilia*), each comprising two infantry regiments each of three battalions; a 94-strong scout *(Esploratori)* unit; an assault *(Arditi)* unit; a machine gun section; a field artillery regiment (five batteries); an engineer battalion (three companies); supply and medical companies. Later, however, the division added other units, including the third line territorial militia *Ivrea* Infantry Brigade, expanding it to about 30,000 men, and thus making it effectively a corps.

In June 1916 Gen. M. K. Dieterichs arrived in Salonika with the 2nd and 4th **Russian** infantry brigades, later joined by the 1st and 3rd and grouped in July 1917 into an 18,000-strong infantry division. A Russian brigade comprised two Special Purpose Regiments (each with four battalions and a machine gun company) formed for overseas service,

Corporal G. Mitchell, Royal Army Service Corps, Corfu, May 1918 in tropical walking-out dress. He is wearing the M1902 Wolseley tropical helmet, 1st pattern KD tunic with shoulder lanyard and an M1874 medical orderly's red cross armband below the RAMC badge (1881-1939) above his worsted rank chevrons. (Nigel Thomas Collection)

French cavalry escort German prisoners to the rear. The cavalrymen are wearing M1915 Cavalry field uniform – horizon-blue field tunic and breeches, (only infantry fought in greatcoats), black leggings and ankle boots and blue Adrian helmet. They wear M1914 belts and ammunition pouches, without supporting straps, carry M1890 cavalry carbines and have their cavalry sabres at the ready. The German infantrymen are wearing M1907 field caps and modified M1910 tunics – and appear happy to be prisoners-of-war. (Dusan Babac Collection)

1st Brigade including a battalion of 1,300 Bosnian volunteers. The Russians were almost continuously in the front line, but were demoralised by the abdication of Tsar Nicholas II in March 1917, and when Gen. Taranovski assumed command in November 1917 the division had been rendered ineffective by communist agitators. In January 1918 the troops were disarmed and interned.

BULGARIA

Bulgaria won independence from Ottoman rule on 13 July 1878. By July 1914 the Kingdom of Bulgaria, under Tsar Ferdinand I, comprised about 5,500,000 Bulgarians with a Turkish minority, covering 48,265 square miles of present Bulgaria plus Eastern Thrace (now Greek). Bulgarian territorial claims on Eastern and Southern Serbia, Rumanian Dobrudja and Greek Western Thrace persuaded Ferdinand to join the Central Powers against the wishes of most of his traditionally pro-Russian subjects.

Troops of a British infantry battalion wearing the khaki drill (KD) tropical service and field uniform worn in Salonika during the hot summer months. The M1902 Wolseley 'foreign service helmet' is worn with the 1st pattern or 2nd pattern KD tunic (with pointed or squared-off pocket flaps respectively) with normal metal and worsted badges from the khaki serge uniform; KD trousers with khaki serge puttees or KD shorts with serge puttees tied at the ankle, or over regimental-colour woollen footless socks called 'hosetops'. The M1902 khaki serge tunic was often combined with the Wolseley helmet and other KD items. The troops are wearing M1908 webbing and some carry the standard .303 SMLE (Short Magazine Lee-Enfield) bolt-action rifle. (Dusan Babac Collection)

Ferdinand was C-in-C of the Bulgarian Army (*Bulgarska Voyska*), with the pro-German Maj. Gen. (later Lt. Gen.) Nikola Zhekov as field commander. From 14 January 1904 the army, with about 390,000 men, was organised in the 85,000-strong First Line Active Army (*Deystvuyushta Armiya*) for men aged 21-23; 250,000-strong Second Line Reserve Army (*Reserna Armiya*) for men aged 24-40; and 54,000-strong Third Line and Fourth Line National Militia (*Narodno Opolecnie*) for men aged 41-44 and 45-46 respectively.

Bulgaria was divided into three Army Regions: 1st (Sofia) – Western Bulgaria; 2nd (Plovdiv) – Southern Bulgaria; 3rd (Ruse) – Northern Bulgaria, plus the 4th (Üskub) in Bulgarian-occupied Serbian Macedonia. Fifteen divisions were raised: two cavalry and 13 infantry (1-13) – the 13th becoming a mountain division in November 1916. These were deployed in four armies: 1st Army (Lt. Gen. Kliment Boyadshiev; 1916 Lt. Gen. Dimit'r Geshov; 1918 Lt. Gen. Stefan Nerezov) in Central Macedonia under Army Group Mackensen; 2nd Army (Lt. Gen. Georgi Todorov; 1917 Maj. Gen. Ivan Lukov) in South-Eastern Macedonia; 3rd Army (1916 Gen. Stefan Toshev, then Lt. Gen. Nerezov; 1917 Maj. Gen., later Lt. Gen. Sava Savov, then Lt. Gen., later Gen. Todorov) in Northern Bulgaria on the Rumanian border, combining with German and Ottoman troops in September 1916 to form the Danube Army in Rumanian Dobrudja; and 4th Army (1918 Lt. Gen. Savov, then Gen. Toshev) in Greek Western Thrace. Six divisions also served in the German 11th Army in South-West Serbia.

A 24,000-strong infantry division – the equivalent of a corps in other armies – comprised two infantry brigades, each with two 4,583-strong infantry regiments containing two 1,057-strong battalions each (a battalion comprising four 263-strong infantry companies), an 80-strong machine gun company and a 180-strong non-combatant labour company; a cavalry battalion (two squadrons); one 1,959-strong field artillery regiment (three three-battery battalions, one howitzer battery); mounted and dismounted military police *(Polska Zhandermeriya)* companies; an engineer battalion (two companies); a medical company; and a supply company. A cavalry division had two cavalry brigades, each with two 657-strong cavalry regiments with four squadrons (a 141-strong squadron including non-combatant labour, machine gun and three cavalry platoons); one horse artillery regiment (with three three-battery battalions); signals, medical and supply companies.

The 1st-3rd Armies each had a heavy artillery, fortress and mountain artillery battalion (three batteries) as headquarters troops. There were 40 first line (1-40) and 35 second line (41-75) infantry regiments – 48 in the 12 infantry divisions, 24 on occupation duties in Macedonia, Morava Region (Eastern Serbia) and Dráma Region (Greek Western Thrace). Thirty-six Third Line National Militia battalions (each with four companies 150-250 strong) also performed occupation duties, while 36 fourth line militia battalions (each with four companies 100-120 strong) were deployed on guard duties in Bulgaria. Army HQ had a Royal Life Guard Cavalry Regiment (three squadrons); twenty-one 148-strong frontier guard companies reassigned from local infantry regiments; a 534-strong railway battalion (four companies); a 537-strong bridging battalion (five companies); a 410-strong signals battalion (three companies); and a mixed engineer and signals battalion. The Army Air Corps *(Vyzduchoplavatelna Druzhina)* manning two squadrons (I-II), formed into a wing in July 1916. The small Bulgarian Navy *(Morski Voyski)*, based at Varna under Maj. Gen.

Bulgarian Army
15 September 1915–30 September 1918

1 Army – 1,6,8,9 Inf.Div (15.9.1915); 8,9 Inf.Div (1916); 5,9, part 11 Inf,13 Mount. Div (9.1918).
2 Army – 2,3,7,11 Inf.Div, 1 Cav.Div (15.9.1915); 7,8,part 11 Inf.Div (9.1918).
3 Army – 4,5,12 Inf.Div. (15.9.1915); 1,4,5,6,12 Inf.Div; 1 Cav.Div (1916).
4 Army – 10 Inf.Div; 2 Cav.Div. (25.11.1917); 10 Inf, 2 Cav. Div (9.1918).
11 German Army – 1,2,3,4,6,12 Inf.Div (9.1918).

1 'Sofia' Infantry Division (Sofia) – Western Bulgaria – 1 Army (10.1915); 3 Army (1916); 11 Army (9.1918). 1/1 Brigade (1,6 Inf.Rgt); 2/1 Brigade (16,25 Inf.Rgt); 4 Art.Regt.
2 'Thrace' Infantry Division (Plovdiv) – Southern Bulgaria – 2 Army (15.9.1915); 11 Army (9.1918). 1/2 Brigade (9,21 Inf.Rgt); 2/2 Brigade (27,28 Inf.Rgt); 3 Art.Regt.
3 'Balkan' Infantry Division (Sliven) – SE. Bulgaria – 2 Army (15.9.1915); 11 Army (9.1918). 1/3 Brigade (11,32 Inf.Rgt); 2/3 Brigade (24,29 Inf.Rgt); 6 Art.Regt.
4 'Preslav' Infantry Division (Shumen) – NE.Bulgaria – 3 Army (15.9.1915); 11 Army (9.1918). 1/4 Brigade (7,19 Inf.Rgt); 2/4 Brigade (8,31 Inf.Rgt); 5 Art.Regt.
5 'Danube' Infantry Division (Ruse) -North-Eastern Bulgaria – 3 Army (15.9.1915); 11 Army (9.1918). 1/5 Brigade (2,5 Inf.Rgt); 2/5 Brigade (18,20 Inf.Rgt); 1 Art.Regt.
6 'Vidin' Infantry Division (Vraca) – N.W. Bulgaria -1 Army (10.1915); 3 Army (1916);11 Army (9.1918). 1/6 Brigade (3,15 Inf.Rgt); 2/6 Brigade (35,36 Inf.Rgt); 2 .Regt.
7 'Rila' Infantry Division (Dubnica) – SW. Bulgaria – 2 Army. 1/7 Brigade (13,26 Inf.Rgt); 2/7 Brigade (14,22 Inf.Rgt); 7 Art.Regt.
8 'Tundzha' Infantry Division (Stara Zagora) – Southern Bulgaria – 1 Army; 2 Army (9.1918). 1/8 Brigade (10,30 Inf.Rgt); 2/8 Brigade (12,23 Inf.Rgt); 8 Art.Regt.
9 'Pleven' Infantry Division (Pleven) – Northern Bulgaria – 1 Army. 1/9 Brigade (4,17 Inf.Rgt); 2/9 Brigade (33,34 Inf.Rgt); 9 Art.Regt.
10 'Black Sea' Infantry Division (Sofia) – Southern Bulgaria – 4 Army. 1/10 Brigade (37,38 Inf.Rgt); 2/10 Brigade (39,40 Inf.Rgt); 10 Art.Regt.
11 'Macedonia' Infantry Division (Sofia) – Serbian Macedonia – 2 Army (15.9.1915); 1/2 Army (9.1918). 1/11 Brigade (1,6 Inf.Rgt); 2/11 Brigade (16,25 Inf.Rgt); 4 Art.Regt.
12 'Ochrid' Infantry Division (Pleven) – Northern Bulgaria – 3 Army (15.9.1915); 11 Army (9.1918). 6,8,9 Depot Rgt,; 4 Art.Regt.
13 Mountain Division – 1 Army (9.1918). 1,2,3 Mount.Rgt; Mount.Art.Rgt; Eng.Coy.
1 Cavalry Division (Sofia). – 2 Army (10.1915); 3 Army (1916). 1 Cav.Brigade (1,5 Cav.Rgt); 4 Cav.Brigade (3,7 Inf.Rgt); 5 Cav.Brigade (5,9 Cav.Rgt); 1 Horse Art.Regt.
2 Cavalry Division (Sofia)- 4 Army. 2 Cav Brigade (4,6 Cav.Rgt); 3 Cav.Brigade (8,10 Cav.Rgt); 2 Horse Art.Regt.

Konstantin Kirkov, with about 500 men manning the *Nadiedja* torpedo-gunboat, six Creusot torpedo-boats and some launches in the Black Sea and Danube Flotillas, had no impact on the war.

Bulgaria's reputation as 'the Prussia of the Balkans' had suffered from her defeat in the 2nd Balkan War (1913), and it required direct German control of half her forces to maintain fighting spirit in Macedonia and Dobrudja in what was an unpopular war. By June 1918 most German troops had been withdrawn from the front line, however, leading to a collapse in morale amongst the war-weary Bulgarians and subsequently to the armistice of 30 September 1918.

GREECE

In February 1821 the Greeks revolted against the Ottoman Empire and on 3 February 1830 had won their independence. By July 1914 Greece, under King Constantine I, included 4,733,013 Greeks, with Turkish and Macedonian Slav minorities, covering 44,759 square miles of present-day Greece less Western Thrace (then Bulgarian) and the Dodecanese Islands (Italian).

Constantine was C-in-C of the Greek Army *(Ellinikos Stratos)*, which was organised into a First Line Active Army for men aged 21-23 years; Second Line Army Reserve for men aged 24-44 years; and Third Line Army Reserve for men aged 45-52 years. Garrison artillery, garrison engineer and signals regiments, and railway, bridging engineer and lorried transport battalions were directly under army headquarters.

Greece was divided into five Military Districts, each recruiting an Army Corps (1-5, in Greek A-E; but the 5th Corps was only partly formed), with 14 divisions (1-14). A corps comprised a 480-man cavalry regiment (5th Corps, a battalion), with four 120-man squadrons; a field artillery regiment with four battalions (5th Corps, three battalions), each with three 153-man batteries; an engineer regiment containing six companies (5th Corps, a battalion with four companies); a transport battalion of three companies (5th Corps, two); a medical battalion; and between two and three divisions. A division (actually an infantry division) comprised three (5th Division, two) infantry and *Evzone* regiments, each with three 1,045-man infantry battalions containing four 253-man rifle companies and a machine gun platoon; and a mountain artillery battalion (three 103-man batteries). There were 41 infantry regiments: 33 line, with five élite Evzone and three Cretan regiments.

The Royal Navy *(Vasilikon Náftikon)* possessed powerful though obsolescent forces comprising five battleships, an armoured cruiser, a light cruiser, 14 destroyers, 14 torpedo-boats and two submarines. The

Army Air Corps *(Ellinikís Polemikís Aeroporias)*, established in September 1912, grew to three squadrons. Additionally the Gendarmerie *(Elliniki Chorofilaki)* comprised 16 dismounted companies and three mounted squadrons.

The Great War divided Greece into King Constantine's neutralist faction, including the Army High Command, which wanted no part in the Great War; and the faction led by the Prime Minister Eleftherios Venizelos, which preferred to join the Entente. Venizelos's offer on 5 March 1915 to send Greek troops to the Dardanelles was vetoed by Constantine, who thereby exceeded his powers as a constitutional monarch. This led Venizelos to resign and initiated a recurrent constitutional crisis – the 'National Schism'. Under the Serbian-Greek Treaty of May 1913 Venizelos mobilised the Greek Army in September 1915 and sanctioned the landing of the *Armée de l'Orient* at Salonika on 5 October. Bulgaria declared war on Greece on 14 October 1915, but Constantine's determined neutrality led to 4th Corps' humiliating surrender of Eastern Macedonia on 18 September 1916. Meanwhile, on 30 August 1916 one Col. Zymbrakakis, with Entente support, staged a coup in Salonika, and on 29 September Venizelos formed a provisional government there, which declared war on the Central Powers on 23 November. In September 1916 Maj. Gen. Zymbrakis established the National Defence Army (later Corps) with 60,000 volunteers. These formed the *Arkhipelagos, Krítis, Séres* and *Kikládes kai Iónia* infantry divisions, named

(continued on page 33)

Greek Army 5 October 1915–11 November 1918

1st ('A') Corps (Athens: Rumelia -Thessaly): 1 Cav.Rgt;1 Field Art.Rgt;1 Eng.Rgt;1 Trans.Bn; Med.Bn.
  I Division (Lárissa, Thessaly) : 4, 5 Inf.Rgt; 1/38 Evzone Rgt; I Mt.Art.Bn.
  II Division (Athens, Western Rumelia) : 1, 7, 34 Inf.Rgt; II Mt.Art.Bn.
  XIII Division (Halkída, Eastern Rumelia) : 2, 3 Inf.Rgt; 5/42 Evzone Rgt; III Mt. Art.Bn.
2nd ('B') Corps (Patras: Peloponese): 2 Cav.Rgt; 3 Field Art.Rgt; 2 Eng.Rgt; 2 Trans.Bn; Med.Bn.
  III Division (Patras: Western Peloponnese) : 6, 12 Inf.Rgt; 2/39 Evzone Rgt; III Mt.Art.Bn.
  IV Division (Náfplio – Eastern Peloponnese) : 8, 11, 35 Inf.Rgt; IV Mt.Art.Bn.
  XIV Division (Kalamáta – Southern Peloponnese) : 9, 36 Inf.Rgt; 1/14 Cretan Rgt; XIV Mt.Art.Bn.
3rd ('C') Corps (Salonika: Macedonia): 3 Cav.Rgt; 5 Field Art.Rgt; 3 Eng.Rgt; 3 Trans.Bn; 3 Med.Bn.
  X Division (Véria – Central Macedonia) : 29, 30 Inf.Rgt; 4/41 Evzone Rgt; X Mt.Art.Bn.
  XI Division (Salonika – Central Macedonia) : 13,27, 28 Inf.Rgt; XI Mt.Art.Bn.
  XII Division (Kozáni – Western Macedonia) : 31 – 33 Inf.Rgt; XII Mt.Art.Bn.
4th('D') Corps (Kavála – Eastern Macedonia): 4 Cav.Rgt;7 Field Art.Rgt;4 Eng.Rgt;4 Trans.Bn; 4 Med.Bn.
  V Division (Dráma – Western Thrace) : 22 Inf.Rgt; 3/37 Cretan Rgt; V Mt.Art.Bn.
  VI Division (Séres – Eastern Macedonia) : 16 – 18 Inf.Rgt; VI Mt.Art.Bn.
  VII Division (Kavála – Western Thrace) : 19, 20 Inf.Rgt; 2/21 Cretan Rgt; VII Mt.Art.Bn.
5th ('E') Corps (Ioánina – Epirus): 5 Cav.Bn; 9 Field Art.Rgt; 5 Eng.Bn; 1 Trans.Bn; 1 Med.Bn.
  VIII Division (Préveza – South Southern Epirus): 10, 15, 24 Inf.Rgt; VIII Mt.Art.Bn.
  IX Division (Ioánina – North Southern Epirus): 25,26,3/40 Evzone Rgt; IX Mt.Art.Bn.
National Defence Army/Corps (Macedonian Front)
  Arkhipelagos Division -1st Group of Divisions.
  Krítis Division – 1st Group of Divisions, later British 16th Corps.
  Séres Division – 1st Group of Divisions, later British 16th Corps.

Army Air Corps:- 531 (Fighter), 532 (Bomber), 533 (Reconnaissance) Squadrons.

A Greek cavalryman, 1916. He wears the M1908 tunic with cavalry breeches and riding boots and has retained the M1908/1910 'German' peaked cap. His M1887 cavalry Other Ranks' sword hangs from his saddle. Cf Plate G3. (Dusan Babac Collection)

THE AUSTRO-HUNGARIAN ARMY
1: Razvodnik, 25th Inf. Regt., 42nd Inf. Div.; Ruma, Western Serbia, August 1914
2: Hauptmann, 3rd Bn., 7th Bosnia-Herzegovinian Inf. Regt., 47th Inf. Div.; Central Albania, August 1918
3: Infanterist, 6th Bn., Albanian Legion; Northern Albania, January 1917

2   3   1

A

THE SERBIAN ARMY
1: Major, 2nd Arty. Regt., Second Line Drina Div.; Belgrade, September 1915
2: Podnarednik, 2nd 'Prince Mihailo' Inf. Regt., First Line Morava Div.; Lesnica, August 1914
3: Kaplar, 19th Inf. Regt., Sumadija Inf. Div.; Vardar Valley, September 1918

2   3   1

B

THE GERMAN & OTTOMAN ARMIES
1: Rittmeister, 11th Dragoon Regt., German 101st Inf. Div.; Vardar Valley, March 1916
2: Oberjäger, Württemberg Mountain Bn.; Transylvanian Alps, October 1916
3: Binbasi, 77th Inf. Regt., 26th Div., Ottoman Army; Kávalla, Western Thrace, March 1917

3

2

1

THE MONTENEGRIN & BRITISH ARMIES
1: Komandir, 7th Mountain Bty., Niksicka Bde.; Western Montenegro, August 1914
2: Desecar, Durmitorska Bde.; Northern Montenegro, September 1915
3: Lance-Corporal, 11th Battalion The Welsh Regt., British 22nd Div.; Battle of Doiran, Macedonia, September 1918

1   2   3

ENTENTE FORCES IN SALONIKA
1: Sergente, Scout Unit, 63rd Inf. Regt., Italian 35th Inf. Div.; Struma Sector, Macedonia, September 1918
2: Sergent, 2bis Zouave Regt., French 11th Colonial Inf. Div.; Monastir Sector, Macedonia, May 1917
3: Shtabs Kapitan, Russian 2nd Bde.; Monastir Sector, Macedonia, May 1917

2   1   3

E

BULGARIAN ARMY
1: Rotmister, 3rd Grand Duchess Maria Krilova Cav. Regt., 1st Cav. Div.; Macedonia, February 1916
2: Feldfebel, 4th Crown Prince Boris Arty. Regt., 4th 'Preslav' Inf. Div.; Dobrudja, September 1916
3: Efreytor, 34th Inf. Regt., 9th 'Pleven' Inf. Div.; Battle of Doiran, September 1918

1   2   3

F

GREEK ARMY
1: Lochagos, Arkhipelagos Div., National Defence Corps; Skrá di Legen,
   Struma Sector, Macedonia, May 1918
2: Lochias, 2/39 Evzone Regt., 3rd Div.; Vetrenik, Crna Sector, Macedonia,
   September 1918
3: Ypodekaneus, 2nd Cav. Regt., 2nd Corps; Doiran Sector, Macedonia,
   September 1918

2   3   1

G

RUMANIAN ARMY
1: Fruntas, 74th Reserve Inf. Regt., 15th Inf. Div.;
   First Battle of Oituz, Western Moldavia, October 1916
2: Sergent major, 3rd Light Inf. Regt., 5th Inf. Div.;
   Battle of Marasesti, Western Moldavia, August 1917
3: Locotenent-colonel, 11th Arty. Regt., 6th Inf. Div.;
   Western Moldavia, November 1918

1   2   3

H

after volunteers' home regions, and the first three divisions fought from December 1916 on the Macedonian Front.

On 10 October 1916 the Entente impounded the Greek Navy and blockaded most of Greece to pressurise Constantine. However, it was an Allied invasion of Thessaly that finally rendered the king's position untenable, and he entered voluntary exile on 12 June 1917. On 27 June 1917 Greece, under Prime Minister Venizelos, declared war on the Central Powers and the navy was returned. By July 1918 a total of 250,000 men in seven divisions had joined the Macedonian front: 1st Corps (1, 2, 13 Inf. Divs.), in Eastern Macedonia; 2nd Corps (3, 4, 14 Inf. Divs.) in the Doiran Sector; and the 9th Infantry Division. These troops acquitted themselves well in the last three months of the war, helping to redeem Greece's reputation with the Entente.

RUMANIA

On 22 May 1866 Moldavia and Wallachia were united as Rumania. By July 1914, under King Ferdinand I, the country comprised some 7,200,000 Rumanians with a small Bulgarian minority, covering 53,945 square miles of present-day Rumania, plus Southern Dobrudja (now Bulgarian), less Hungarian Transylvania and Eastern Banat and Austrian Bukovina.

From 6 May 1913 the Rumanian Armed Forces *(Armata Românâ)* comprised the army *(Trupe de uscat)* and Royal Navy *(Marina Regala)*. The First Line Active Army *(Armata Activa)* was for men aged 21-28, Second Line Reserve *(Reserva Armatei)* for the ages 29-40, and Third Line Militia *(Militii)* for the ages 41-46. Ferdinand was C-in-C with Gen. Dumutru Iliescu as Chief of Staff. On 27 August 1916 the army mobilised 833,601 troops in 20 first and second line infantry divisions and two cavalry divisions (1-2). Second line divisions 21-23 were formed on 9 September. The divisions were grouped into seven corps (1-7), forming: 1st Army (Craiova) in North-Western Wallachia under Lt. Gen. Ioan Clucer, then Maj. Gen. Ion Dragalina; 2nd Army (Baicoi) in Southern Moldavia under Lt. Gen. Grigore Crainiceanu, then Lt. Gen. Alexandru Averescu; 3rd Army (Bucharest) in Southern Wallachia under Averescu; Northern (later 4th) Army (Bacau) in Northern Moldavia under Lt. Gen. Constantin Presan; with 5 Corps in strategic reserve.

Rumanian Army 15 August 1916–30 April 1917/ 1 May 1917/10 November 1918

1 Army:- 1 Corps; 1 *Cal*.Brig. (1,2 *Cal*. Rgt). / 3,5,6,Cav.Corps.
2 Army:- 2 Corps; 3 Corps; 3 *Cal*.Brig. (5,6 *Cal*.Rgt). / 2,4 Corps; 1 Cav.Div; 1 *Cal*.Brig;Front.Brig.
3 Army:- 6 Corps; 7 Corps; 2 *Cal*.Brig. (3,4 *Cal*.Rgt).
Northern/4 Army:- 4 Corps; 2 Cav.Div; 4 *Cal*.Brig. (7,8 *Cal*.Cav.Rgt).

1 Corps (Craiova):- 1,2,11-13,20,23 Inf.Div. // (Bacau):- 1,2,11 Inf.Div.
2 Corps (Bucharest):- 3,4 Inf.Div. /(Ploiesti):- 1,3,12 Inf.Div / (Cetatea Alba):- 3,4,12 Inf.Div.
3 Corps (Galati):- 5,6,22 Inf.Div. /(Rîmnicu Sarat):- 5,9,13 Inf.Div. / (Galati):- 5,6,13 Inf.Div.
4 Corps (Iasi):- 7,8,14 Inf.Div. /(Bacau):- 6-8 Inf.Div. / (Iasi):- 7,8,14 Inf.Div.
5 Corps (Constanta):- 10,15,21 Inf.Div. / (Braila):- 10,14 Inf.Div. / (Chisinau):- 9,10,15 Inf.Div.
6 Corps (Oltenita):- 16,18 Inf.Div; 1 Cav.Div. / 15 Inf, 2 Cav.Div.
7 Corps (Dubruja):- 9,17,19 Inf.Div; 5 Cal.Brig. (9,10 Cal.Rgt).
Cavalry Corps (1917):- 1,6 *Ros,* 1 *Cal.* Brig.
Air Corps:- 1 Wing(N1,F2,F6 Sqn); 2 Wing(N3,F4 Sqn); 3 Wing(F5,N10 Sqn); 4 Wing(F7,B8 Sqn).
1 Inf.Div. (Turnu Severin):- 1 Inf.Brig. (17,57/18 Inf.Rgt); 2 Inf.Brig. (16/1,25/31 Inf.Rgt); 31/- Inf.
  Brig. (43,59 Inf.Rgt); 1 Lt.Inf.Rgt; 1 Art.Brig. (1 Art,5 Art/How.Rgt);-/2 *Cal*.Rgt; -/1 Eng.Bn.
2 Inf.Div. (Craiova):- 4 Inf.Brig. (3,19 Inf.Rgt); 32 Inf.Brig. (26,66 Inf.Rgt);/ 3 Inf.Brig.
  (2, 26 Inf.Rgt) /; 5 Lt.Inf.Rgt; 2 Art.Brig.(9 Art,14 Art/How.Rgt); -/2 *Cal*.Rgt; -/2 Eng.Bn.
3 Inf.Div. (Tirgoviste):- 5 Inf.Brig. (4,28 Inf.Rgt); 6 Inf. Brig. (22,30 Inf.Rgt); 33/- Inf.Brig.
  (1,45 Inf.Rgt); 2 Lt.Inf.Rgt; 3 Art.Brig. (6 Art,15 Art/How.Rgt); -/4 *Cal*.Rgt; -/3 Eng.Bn.
4 Inf.Div. (Bucharest):- 7 Inf.Brig. (5,20 Inf.Rgt); 8 Inf. Brig. (6,21 Inf.Rgt); 34/- Inf.Brig. (46,61
  Inf.Rgt); 6 Lt.Inf.Rgt; 4 Art.Brig. (2 Art,10 Art/How.Rgt); -/4 *Cal*.Rgt; -/4 Eng.Bn.
5 Inf.Div. (Buzau):- 9 Inf.Brig. (7,32 Inf.Rgt); 10 Inf. Brig. (8,9 Inf.Rgt); 35/- Inf.Brig. (50,64 Inf.Rgt);
  3 Lt.Inf.Rgt; 5 Art.Brig. (7 Art, 3 Art/19 How.Rgt); -/6 *Cal*.Rgt; -/5 Eng.Bn.
6 Inf.Div. (Focsani):- 11 Inf.Brig. (10,24 Inf.Rgt); 12 Inf. Brig. (11,12 Inf.Rgt); 36/- Inf.Brig.
  (51,52 Inf.Rgt); 4/7 Lt.Inf.Rgt; 6 Art.Brig. (11Art,16 Art/How.Rgt); -/6 *Cal*.Rgt; -/6 Eng.Bn.
7 Inf.Div. (Roman):- 13 Inf.Brig. (15,27 Inf.Rgt); 14 Inf. Brig. (14,16 Inf.Rgt); 37/- Inf. Brig. (14,16
  Inf.Rgt); 7/4 Lt.Inf.Rgt; 7 Art.Brig. (4 Art,8 Art/How.Rgt); -/8 *Cal*.Rgt; -/7 Eng.Bn.
8 Inf.Div. (Botosani):- 15 Inf.Brig. (13,25 Inf.Rgt); 16 Inf.Brig. (29, 37 Inf.Rgt); 38/- Inf. Brig.
  (53,65 Inf.Rgt); 8 Lt.Inf.Rgt; 8 Art.Brig. (12 Art,17 Art/How.Rgt); -/8 *Cal*.Rgt; -/8 Eng.Bn.
9 Inf.Div. (Silistra):- 19/18 Inf.Brig. (35,23/36,63/- Inf.Rgt); /17 Inf.Brig. (34,40 Inf.Rgt);
  7/9 Lt.Inf. Rgt; 9 Art.Brig. (13 Art,18 Art/How.Rgt); -/10 *Cal*.Rgt; -/9 Eng.Bn.
10 Inf.Div. (Tulcea):- 40/19 Inf. Brig. (38/23,78/39 Inf.Rgt); 20 Inf.Brig. (33,73/38 Inf.Rgt);
  10 Lt.Inf.Rgt; 10 Art.Brig. (3 Art,20 Art/How.Rgt); -/10 *Cal*.Rgt; -/10 Eng.Bn.
11 Inf.Div.:- 21 Inf.Brig. (18/43-59,58/66-42 Inf.Rgt); 22 Inf. Brig. (41/41-71,71/57-58 Inf.Rgt);
  11 Art.Brig. (21 Art,26-1 Art/How.Rgt); -/2 *Cal*.Rgt; -/11 Eng.Bn.
12 Inf.Div.:- 23 Inf.Brig. (60/45-60,68/46-61 Inf.Rgt); 24 Inf. Brig. (62/44-68,70/62-70 Inf.Rgt);
  12 Art.Brig. (22 Art,27-2 Art/How.Rgt); -/4 *Cal*.Rgt; -/12 Eng.Bn.
13 Inf.Div.:- 25 Inf.Brig. (47/50-64,72/51-52 Inf.Rgt); 26 Inf. Brig. (48/48-49,49/47-72 Inf.Rgt);
  13 Art.Brig. (23 Art,28-3 Art/How.Rgt); -/6 *Cal*.Rgt; -/3 Eng.Bn.
14 Inf.Div.:- 27 Inf.Brig. (55/69-77,67/53-65 Inf.Rgt); 28 Inf. Brig. (54/55-67,56/54-56 Inf.Rgt);
  31/- Inf.Brig. (43,59 Inf.Rgt); 14 Art.Brig. (24 Art,29-4 Art/How.Rgt); -/8 *Cal*.Rgt; -/14 Eng.Bn.
15 Inf.Div.:- 28/29 Inf.Brig. (74/63-79 Inf.Rgt); 30 Inf. Brig. (75/75-76,80/74-80 Inf.Rgt);
  15 Art.Brig. (25 Art,30-5 Art/How.Rgt); -/10 *Cal*.Rgt; -/15 Eng.Bn.
16 Inf.Div.:- 43 Mixed Brig. (20,60 Inf.Rgt). 44 Mixed Brig. (5,45 Inf.Rgt).
17 Inf.Div.:- 18 Inf.Brig. (36,76 Inf.Rgt); 39 Inf. Brig. (75,79,80 Inf.Rgt).
18 Inf. Div:- 2 Mixed Brig. (2 Frontier,62,68 Inf.Rgt); 3 Mixed Brig. (10,48-50 Inf.Rgt).
19 Inf. Div:- 5 Mixed Brig. (39,40 Inf.Rgt); 6 Mixed Brig. (6 bns from 11,12,24,51,52,64 Inf.Rgt).
20 Inf. Div:- 41 Mixed Brig. (1,26,41,58,66,71 Terr.Bn); 1 Mixed Brig. (3,19,42,43,59 Terr.Bn).
21 Inf. Div:- 33 Inf. Brig. (45, & 3bns from 30,44,70 Inf.Rgt); 34 Inf.Brig. (46,61 Inf.Rgt).
22 Inf. Div:- 9 Inf.Brig. (7,32 Inf.Rgt); 35 Inf. Brig. (50,64 Inf.Rgt).
23 Inf. Div:- 3 Inf.Brig. (2,42 Inf.Rgt); Combined Brig. (44 Inf, 1 Frontier Rgt).
1 Light. Div:- 1,4-6 Lt.Inf.Rgt; 2 Art,1 Mt.Art,1 How.Bty; 1 *Cal*.Sqn.
2 Light. Div:- 2-3,7-10 Lt.Inf.Rgt; 2 Art,1 Mt.Art,1 How.Bty; 1 *Cal.* Sqn.
1 Cav.Div (Bucharest):- 1 *Ros*.Brig. (1,10 *Ros*.Rgt); 5 *Ros*.Brig. (4,9 *Ros.*.Rgt); 6 *Ros*.Brig.
  (11,12 *Ros*.Rgt); 1 Horse Art.Bn.
2 Cav.Div (Iasi):- 2 *Ros*.Brig.(2,3 *Ros*.Rgt); 3 *Ros*.Brig.(5,6 *Ros*.Rgt); 4 *Ros.*.Brig.(7,8 *Ros*.Rgt);
  2 Horse Art.Bn.

A Bulgarian infantryman wearing the M1908 Other Ranks' coarse quality natural-coloured cloth greatcoat, double-breasted, but with only one row of six brown metal buttons down the centre, and red Russian-style collar patches. The black-peaked cap has infantry red piping, cap band and black leather chin strap. He is wearing M1908 black leather infantry equipment and carries an M1895 Mannlicher 8mm bolt-action rifle. Cf Plate F3. (Dusan Babac Collection)

A 27,000-strong first line infantry division (1-10) comprised: two infantry brigades (each of two active regiments) and a reserve infantry brigade. A 4,793-strong regiment comprised three 1,160-strong infantry battalions, each with three four-platoon companies, and a machine gun company; a light infantry *(Vinatori)* regiment, two battalions. The division also had a *Calarasi* squadron; an artillery brigade with two field regiments each with two three-battery battalions; three 5.3cm artillery support batteries; an engineer company, a signals 'section' (half-platoon); and a service battalion (medical company, supply column, ammunition column). A second line infantry division (11-15) had two reserve infantry brigades, while other second line divisions (16-23) had two first or second line brigades or 'mixed infantry brigades' with an infantry regiment's 4th Territorial Battalion and militia battalions, plus an artillery brigade and cavalry battalion (two squadrons). Infantry brigades 1-20 and regiments 1-40 were first line, and brigades 21-40 and regiments 41-80 were second line reserve units. A 5,280-strong Cavalry Division comprised three two-regiment cavalry brigades, each 746-strong regiment having four cavalry squadrons and a machine gun section; a cyclist detachment; a horse artillery battalion (three 189-strong batteries); radio and telegraph half-platoons; and a service battalion. Line cavalry was styled *Rosiori* ('Red Men'), and territorial reserve cavalry, *Calarasi* (Cavalry). There was also a Royal Bodyguard Regiment (of three squadrons), a Frontier Guard Brigade and a Volunteer Motor Corps. The Corps of Mountain Infantry *(Vinatori de Munte)*, formed on 16 November 1915, was by 1916 a 1,980-strong regiment with three battalions, each battalion having one machine gun, one telegraph and four rifle companies.

The army suffered 29 per cent losses (240,000 men) in 1916 from its badly under-equipped and under-officered mass infantry divisions. In April 1917 the 700,000-man Rumanian Army, now cornered in Eastern Moldavia behind the Seret

The commander and senior officers of the Bulgarian 10th Infantry Division, 1916. All are wearing the M1915 superior quality officers' grey-green plain peaked cap, service tunic, breeches and black riding boots. (Nigel Thomas Collection)

Two Bulgarian infantry officers in M1908 officers' superior quality grey-green service and field uniforms. Both are wearing Russian-pattern silver belts with red and green threads (replaced in 1915 by a leather belt), and are carrying standard equipment – M1889 officers' sabres, revolvers in holsters with coloured lanyards, binocular cases and map cases. The officer on the left is wearing the white silk aiguillettes of an officer attached to the General Staff or an aide-de-camp to a general officer. (Dusan Babac Collection)

A group of Greek *Evzones,* May 1918. The five élite Evzone regiments were used as assault troops, but incurred such heavy losses in the two Balkan and two World Wars that they were disbanded in 1944, leaving a Royal (from June 1973 Presidential) Guard only. The soldier at left is wearing the M1915 khaki *doulama* tunic with M1908 fez (without tassel) and heavy yellow-edged Evzone khaki cape, his non-regulation but widely worn waistbelt and shoulder belt hold ammunition for his M1903 Austro-Hungarian Schönauer 6.5mm rotary-magazine rifle. See Plate G2. (Dusan Babac Collection)

River with Gen. Presan as Chief of Staff, was placed under Russian strategic command (Gen. Vladimir Zaharov, later Gen. Dimitri Sherbatsev). French Gen. Henri Mathias Berthelot's Military Mission reorganised the Rumanian Army into 15 first line infantry and two cavalry divisions deployed in five corps (2-6) and a cavalry corps (1 *Calarasi*, 1, 6 dismounted *Rosiori* Brigades). These were allocated to 1st Army (Gen. Constantin Cristescu, then Lt. Gen. Eremia Grigorescu) and 2nd Army (Gen. Averescu) with three divisions (2, 4, 11) in army reserve.

Infantry divisions had reduced manpower but increased firepower: an infantry regiment added a 4th supply company; four supernumerary infantry or light infantry militia battalions replaced the reserve infantry brigade; divisional cavalry doubled to a battalion (two squadrons); one field artillery regiment of the artillery brigade became a howitzer regiment (two two-battery battalions), a trench-mortar battery was added with only one 5.3cm field battery; engineers expanded to a battalion (engineer, bridging, signals, rocket companies); a military police (*Jandarmeria*) detachment was added, as was a mobile hospital to the service battalion. A cavalry division reduced its line cavalry to one mounted *Rosiori* brigade (two four-squadron regiments) and a

Rumanian gunners, 1917. The crew of the Rumanian M1896 Vikers 127mm howitzer are wearing M1915 field uniforms with Adrian helmets while the officers (left background) are wearing a variety of field tunics. Note that by 1917 the black officers' breeches were no longer compulsory. (Horia Serbanescu Collection)

dismounted *Rosiori* regiment. It also expanded its cyclists to a company, dropped the telegraph half-platoon and added an MP detachment. In addition there was a Mountain Infantry Corps; a Frontier Guard Brigade (two three-battalion regiments, 5.3cm battery); two two-regiment Garrison ('Fortress') Artillery brigades; two seven-battery Mountain Artillery regiments; railway, bridging, garrison and specialist engineer battalions.

In August 1916 the Rumanian Navy (HQ Galati) disbanded its Sea Division, leaving the Danube Division's flotilla of four armoured monitors, four gunboats and eight torpedo-boats to confront the Austro-Hungarian Danube Flotilla. The Army Air Corps *(Corpul Aerian Romana)* was formed on 20 April 1913, and on 15 August 1916 assigned a mixed squadron *(escadrila)* to each numbered army, with a wing *(grup)* defending Bucharest. In January 1917 the corps was expanded into four mixed wings (1-4) each with two or three squadrons, and in March 1917 redesignated Royal Rumanian Aviation *(Aeronautica Regala Romana).*

From August 1916 to December 1917 the **Russian** army supported Rumania with 44 divisions. In Bukovina and Northern Moldavia there was 9th Army (40 Corps) in 1916, 8th in 1917; in Southern Moldavia the 4th Army (7, 8 Corps) in 1916, 9th (2, 24, 26, 36, 40 Corps) in 1917; in Eastern Wallachia the 4th Army (7, 8, 30 Corps) in 1917; in Dobrudja the Danube Army (47 Corps) in 1916, 6th Army (4, 47, 4 Siberian, 6 Cav. Corps) in 1917. The Army Reserve comprised 29, 45, and 3 Cav. Corps in 1917.

Rumania delayed implementing demobilisation of the army, as required by the Treaty of Bucharest of 7 May 1918, reorganising into five corps, each with three infantry divisions. On 10 November 1918 the army, now under Gen. Cristescu, remobilised seven infantry divisions (6-10, 13-14), two cavalry divisions (1-2) and two new light divisions (1-2); and by 1 December 1918 had occupied Transylvania, Eastern Banat, Bukovina and Southern Dobrudja, doubling the size of Rumania to 113,887 square miles.

A Rumanian soldier, Eastern Moldavia, spring 1917, wearing ragged and improvised equipment typical of an army which had suffered heavy defeats the previous year. He has a Rumanian M1915 gasmask – a grey wool hood impregnated with sodium thiosulphate – Rumania also used the French M2 and Russian 'Zelinsky-Cummaut' models. He also wears a civilian *touloupe* sheepskin coat over his field tunic, and he is using string instead of supporting straps for his loaded M1891 leather ammunition pouches. He carries the standard Rumanian M1893 Mannlicher 6.5mm bolt-action rifle. (Horia Serbanescu Collection)

THE PLATES

A: THE AUSTRO-HUNGARIAN ARMY

A1: Razvodnik, 25th Infantry Regiment, 42nd Infantry Division; Ruma, Western Serbia, August 1914

Josip 'Tito' Broz, prime minister, later president, of Yugoslavia March 1945-May 1980, served in the Hungarian *Honvédség* during September 1913-June 1917. He wears the coarse quality Other Ranks' summer M1908 'pike-grey' *(hechtgrau)* uniform, introduced 7 October 1908. The unstiffened peaked field cap bears the Hungarian 'IFJ' (Franz-Josef I) badge. The tunic has *Honvédség* infantry 'slate-grey' collar patches with rank star on the low collar. Hungarian belt plate; Hungarian dismounted trousers with slate-grey knots; M1909 brown cowhide equipment, and standard M1895 Mannlicher 8mm bolt-action rifle.

A2: Hauptmann, 3rd Bn, 7th Bosnia-Herzegovinian Infantry Regiment, 47th Infantry Division; Central Albania, August 1918

The 'pike-grey' uniform was replaced from 13 September 1915 by a German *feldgrau* uniform, in 1918 officially superseded by brown-grey. This captain wears a standard Moslem field fez (also widely worn by Christians) with semi-official campaign badges. His M1915 officer's field tunic has a high stand-and-fall collar with rank stars, the red branch-colour collar patch reduced in 1917 to a strip. He has an Other Ranks' belt plate with an Austrian eagle, officers' breeches and gaiters, the M1912 Steyr-Hahn 9mm automatic pistol and an M1895 bayonet.

A3: Infanterist, 6th Battalion, Albanian Legion; Northern Albania, January 1917

This private, in a company attached to an Austro-Hungarian infantry battalion, wears the traditional Northern Albanian large white lambswool *keçe* skullcap (later replaced by a field-grey fez with red-black-red cockade); and the M1915 coarse quality Other Ranks' uniform and greatcoat. He has an M1917 canvas rucksack, M1909 brown cowhide equipment, and an M1890 Landsturm bolt-action rifle.

B: THE SERBIAN ARMY

B1: Major, 2nd Artillery Regiment, Second Line Drina Division; Belgrade, September 1915

In accordance with uniform regulations of 5 May 1911 this officer wears the M1908 officer's grey-green *(sivo-maslinasta)* superior quality service and field uniform. Note the Order of the White Eagle 5th Class, and the M1861 artillery officer's sabre. The soft or stiffened service cap, copied from the *sajkaca* peakless 19th century frontier guard's cap, has a gum-covered non-reflecting peak, and an M1904 officer's oval cockade with a royal monogram. Subaltern officers had branch-colour, field officers gold gimp crown piping, field marshals and general officers adding a gold braid flap edging; NCOs wore a plain cap with cockade only. The tunic has a branch-colour cloth (general staff, artillery, engineers – velvet) collar and cuff piping; the greatcoat a branch-colour spearhead collar patch, collar, pocket flap and cuff piping, with red cloth lapels for the rank of major and above. Branch-colour piped breeches were worn with black leather riding boots or brown ankle boots and leather gaiters. Field marshals and general officers had gold greatcoat collar patches and double red cloth breeches

stripes. Second line troops often wore the dark blue M1896 uniform, third line troops a military cap and greatcoat with civilian clothes.

B2: Podnarednik, 2nd 'Prince Mihailo' Infantry Regiment, First Line Morava Division; Lesnica, August 1914

This 'Iron Regiment' NCO wears the M1908 Other Ranks' cloth service and field uniform, his peakless field cap omitting the NCO's plain cockade in the field; officers wore a cockade with monogram and service cap pipings and braids. His tunic has branch-colour rectangular cloth collar patches; loose breeches, tight from the knee, were worn with traditional woollen socks and *opanci* shoes when black marching boots were unavailable. His M1908 greatcoat, with rectangular branch-colour collar patches, is rolled over his shoulder. He has brown leather equipment with M1895 German ammunition pouches, a slung waterbottle and canvas bag, and a 7mm Mauser-Koka-Djuric M1880/1907 rifle and bayonet.

B3: Kaplar, 19th Infantry Regiment, Sumadija Infantry Division; Vardar Valley, September 1918

Most officers in the reconstituted Serbian Army in Salonika retained their M1908 uniform, sometimes made from British or French khaki. Others, and all Other Ranks, were issued the M1915 French 'horizon blue' field uniform; the M1915 French African Army khaki version illustrated (both with added shoulder straps); or the M1902 British service dress uniform. This section machine-gunner wears the French M1915 Adrian helmet with Serbian badge, and displays the Karageorge Star in gold with swords for bravery. He carries an automatic pistol and a French M1915 'Chauchat' light machine gun. The Serbian Volunteer Corps wore Russian uniforms.

C: THE GERMAN & OTTOMAN ARMIES

C1: Rittmeister, 11th Dragoon Regiment, German 101st Infantry Division; Vardar Valley, March 1916

This captain wears the M1908 superior quality greenish-grey *feldgrau* Prussian cavalry field uniform with the 11th Dragoons' crimson regimental distinctions. The M1910 peaked service cap has a regimental cap band and crown piping, with national red-white-black above Prussian black-white-black cockades. He wears an M1908 Dragoon tunic modified on 3 March 1915 with plain turnback cuffs, but has retained regimental piping and added an M1915 (3 September) collar. The M1915 matt silver-grey wire shoulder straps show rank, regimental underlay and number. He wears M1908 reinforced cavalry breeches with standard blackened M1915 cavalry riding boots; carries an officer's map case, 10 x 50 Zeiss binoculars, and a P08 Luger automatic pistol; and displays the 1914 Iron Cross 1st Class.

C2: Oberjäger, Württemberg Mountain Battalion; Transylvanian Alps, October 1916

This corporal in Oberleutnant Erwin Rommel's unit wears the Württemberg ranker's ski tunic introduced 2 October 1915. The collar patches, with silver rank braid and company number button, the collar piping and the distinctive shoulder welts are in light infantry green. He wears an M1907 standard Other Ranks' field cap with green cap band and crown piping, with the black-red-black Württemberg and national cockades; M1914 baggy ski trousers, studded climbing

Officers wear shoulder boards on the grey-green M1908 service tunic and greatcoat, Other Ranks stars on the grey-green uniform shoulder straps. The same insignia is worn on French and British uniforms on the Salonika Front.

Field marshals and general officers *(vojvode i generali)* **(1-3)**:- gold braid cords, gold buttons, grey-blue underlay, silver metal eagle and monogram. Field officers *(visi oficiri)* **(4-7)**:- gold (silver - 5,7) braid shoulder board, gold (silver - 5,7) buttons, branch-colour piping, silver (gold - 5,7) metal pips and unit insignia. Subaltern officers *(nizi oficiri)* **(8-12)**:- gold (silver - 9-12) braid shoulder-board, gold (silver - 9-12) buttons, branch-colour piping, silver (gold - 9-12) metal pips and unit insignia. Non-commissioned officers *(Podoficiri)*, men *(kaplari i redovi)* **(13-18)**:-grey-green uniform strap, gold (silver - 13,15) buttons, gold metal pips and unit insignia.

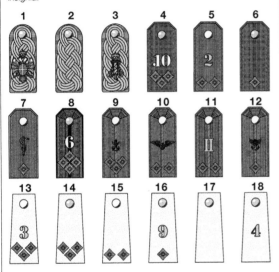

1. Vojvoda *(Field Marshal)*
2. Djeneral *(Maj. Gen.)*
3. Djeneral *(Maj. Gen.)* King's Adjutant
4. Pukovnik *(Colonel)* 10th Infantry Regt.
5. Potpukovnik *(Lt. Col.)* 2nd Cavalry Regt.
6. Major *(Major)* General Staff.

7. Major *(Major)* Medical Corps
8. Kapetan I klase *(Senior Captain)* 6th Field Artillery Regt.
9. Kapetan II klase *(Captain)* Bridging Engineer Bn.
10. Porucnik *(Lieutenant)* Railway Engineer Bn.
11. Porucnik *(Lieutenant)* 2nd Garrison Artillery Bn.
12. Potporucnik *(2nd Lieutenant)* Air Corps

13. Narednik *(Sergeant)* 3rd Engineer Bn.
14. Narednik *(Sergeant)* Serbian Volunteer Corps
15. Podnarednik *(Corporal)* Timok/1 Cavalry Regt.
16. Kaplar *(Lance-Corporal)* 9th Mountain Artillery Battery
17. Redov *(Private)* Frontier Troops
18. Redov *(Private)* 4th Infantry Regt.

boots and puttees; M1909 leather belt (with Württemberg buckle), infantry support Y-straps and ammunition pouches, ordered blackened in September 1915. He carries a 7.92mm Karabiner 98 rifle, and displays the 1914 Iron Cross 2nd Class ribbon.

C3: Binbasi, 77th Infantry Regiment, 26th Division, Ottoman Army; Kávalla, Western Thrace, March 1917

This major wears an officer's superior quality M1909 khaki service and field uniform with a *kabalak* field cap with officer's branch-colour piping. The tunic with officers' pointed flaps has a branch-colour collar, gold buttons and German-style shoulder boards in gold with silver pentagonal rank pips, also worn on the light grey greatcoat with branch-colour collar. He wears the German 1914 Iron Cross ribbon and the Ottoman War Medal breast star, and carries a German 7.63mm Mauser C96 automatic pistol.

D: THE MONTENEGRIN & BRITISH ARMIES
D1: Komandir, 7th Mountain Battery, Niksicka Brigade; Western Montenegro, August 1914

On 3 October 1910 the Montenegrin Army replaced the national dress uniform with a Russian-style khaki service uniform, modified on 3 April 1914 with Serbian features to emphasis Balkan War solidarity. This battery commander wears the superior quality officers' service dress with M1910 peaked cap and M1871 cap badge. The M1910 tunic had Russian shoulder boards, plain open collar and cuffs, modified in April 1914 with a Serbian-style closed stand-up branch-coloured collar and cuff piping – artillery having a black collar. His M1910 officers' breeches have branch-colour piping – general officers a wide gold braid stripe, in April 1914 double crimson stripes. He wears the Russian General Staff Academy breast badge and carries officer's binoculars, leather map case and an ornate M1870 9mm Gasser-Montenegrin pistol. In full dress uniform officers wore epaulettes, in field uniform a 'pillbox' cap and no shoulder boards. King's adjutants and staff officers wore gold (orderly officers, silver) wire aiguillettes on the right shoulder, both in khaki on the field uniform. The M1910 officer's khaki double-breasted six-buttoned greatcoat had branch-colour rectangular collar patches with a button, general officers and *komandir* adding red cloth lapels.

D2: Desecar, Durmitorska Brigade; Northern Montenegro, September 1915

This section commander wears the standard Other Ranks' M1910 khaki service and field uniform. His tunic, worn with a khaki cloth sash, has no insignia; the single M1910 branch-colour shoulder strap loop was never worn. He wears baggy trousers cut tight from the knee, civilian *opanci* shoes and Russian M1893 leather equipment. He has the Silver Medal for Bravery, and carries a Russian M1891 '3-line' Moisin-Nagant 'Moskovska' 7.61mm rifle.

D3: Lance-Corporal, 11th Battalion The Welsh Regiment, British 22nd Division; Battle of Doiran, Macedonia, September 1918

This platoon machine-gunner wears the Other Ranks' khaki serge service dress uniform introduced January 1902. The tunic has shoulder straps with the brass WELSH (changing to WELCH on 1 January 1921) title and black loop divisional battle insignia; sleeve rank chevrons; on the right cuff service chevrons for four years' overseas service since August 1914,

Branch and unit distinctions of the Serbian Army
29 July 1914 - 11 November 1918

Branch	Officer's collar [1]	Other Ranks' collar-patch	Officers' shoulder-board [2]	Unit insignia
General-officers	grey-blue cloth	–	gold	–
King's Adjutants and King's Orderly Officers	branch	–	branch	Royal monogram [4]
General Staff officers	red velvet	–	gold	–
9 1st Line infantry regiments	dark red cloth	dark red cloth	gold	3,14,17,19,20-24
1st 'Prince Milos the Great' Infantry Regiment	dark red cloth	dark red cloth	gold	1
2nd 'Prince Mihailo' Infantry Regiment	dark red cloth	dark red cloth	gold	2
4th 'Stevan Nemanja' Infantry Regiment	dark red cloth	dark red cloth	gold	4
5th 'King Milan' Infantry Regiment	dark red cloth	dark red cloth	gold	5
6th 'Crown Prince Aleksandar' Infantry Regt.	dark red cloth	dark red cloth	gold	6
7th 'King Petar' Infantry Regiment	dark red cloth	dark red cloth	gold	7
8th 'Prince Aleksandar' Infantry Regiment	dark red cloth	dark red cloth	gold	8
9th 'King Nikola I' Infantry Regiment	dark red cloth	dark red cloth	gold	9
10th 'Tarkov' Infantry Regiment	dark red cloth	dark red cloth	gold	10
11th 'Karadjordje' Infantry Regiment	dark red cloth	dark red cloth	gold	11
12th 'Tsar Lazar' Infantry Regiment	dark red cloth	dark red cloth	gold	12
13th 'Hajduk Veljko' Infantry Regiment	dark red cloth	dark red cloth	gold	13
15th 'Stevan Sindjelic' Infantry Regiment	dark red cloth	dark red cloth	gold	15
16th 'Tsar Nikolai II Romanov' Infantry Regt.	dark red cloth	dark red cloth	gold	16
18th 'Prince Djordje' Infantry Regiment	dark red cloth	dark red cloth	gold	18
6 Serbian Volunteer Corps infantry regiments	dark red cloth	dark red cloth	gold	–
19 supernumerary infantry regiments	dark red cloth	dark red cloth	gold	–
Royal Guard Regiment	dark blue cloth	dark blue cloth	gold braid	silver crown
1st 'Milos Obilic' Cavalry Regiment	dark blue cloth	dark blue cloth	silver/gold [3]	1
2nd 'Tsar Dusan' Cavalry Regiment	dark blue cloth	dark blue cloth	silver/gold [3]	2
3rd Cavalry Regiment	dark blue cloth	dark blue cloth	silver/gold [3]	3
4th 'Grand Duke Konstantin Konstantinovich' Cavalry Regt.	dark blue cloth	dark blue cloth	silver/gold [33]	4
7 1st Line divisional cavalry regiments	dark blue cloth	dark blue cloth	silver/gold [3]	–
5 2nd Line divisional cavalry regiments	dark blue cloth	dark blue cloth	silver/gold [3]	–
19 divisional field artillery regiments	black velvet	black cloth	gold	1 – 6
1 Heavy Artillery Regiment	black velvet	red-black diagonal cloth	gold	–
2 Garrison Artillery battalions	black velvet	black-red diagonal cloth	gold	I – II
1 Horse Artillery Regiment	black velvet	black cloth, red horizontal stripe	gold	–
9 Mountain Artillery batteries	black velvet	black cloth, red vertical stripe	gold	1 – 9
12 Ammunition columns	black velvet	black cloth	gold	–
6 Engineer battalions	cherry red cloth	cherry red cloth	silver/gold [3]	1 – 6
1 Railway Engineer Battalion	cherry red cloth	cherry red cloth	silver/gold [3]	winged wheel
1 Bridging Engineer Battalion	cherry red cloth	cherry red cloth	silver/gold [3]	fouled anchor, oars
Pigeon Post	cherry red cloth	cherry red cloth	silver/gold [3]	winged envelope
6 Air Corps (Vazduhoplovne komande) sqns.	cherry red cloth	cherry red cloth	silver/gold [3]	fouled anchor, wings
12 Supply columns	grey cloth	grey cloth	silver/gold [3]	–
Bandsmen		original branch	–	collar patch lyre
Medical officers	brown velvet	–	silver/gold [3]	snake & staff
12 Medical Company personnel	brown cloth	–	–	–
Veterinary officers	brown velvet	–	silver/gold [3]	snake, staff, horseshoe
Pharmaceutical officers	brown velvet	–	silver/gold [3]	snake & goblet
Legal officers	purple cloth	–	silver/gold [3]	–
25 Frontier Troops companies	green cloth	green cloth	gold	(white collar star)
5 Gendarmerie (Zandarmerija) battalions	dark red cloth	dark red cloth	gold	(white collar star)
Gornjac, Jadar, Rudnik, Zlatibor guerilla Chetnik detachments	Civilian clothing			

Notes

1 The same colour appeared as cloth piping on the service peaked cap, service tunic and greatcoat, shoulder boards and greatcoat collar patches.

2 Also the button-colour.

3 The button-colour changed to gold in July 1916.

4 King's Adjutants could be general officers or field officers; King's Orderly Officers were field officers.

and on the left a single wound stripe and a two years' good conduct chevron. He wears the M1916 Mk I helmet, M1914 machine-gunner's leather equipment and M1917 'small box respirator' gasmask, and carries a Mk I Lewis light machine gun.

E: ENTENTE FORCES IN SALONIKA

E1: Sergente, Scout Unit, 63rd Infantry Regiment, Italian 35th Infantry Division; Struma Sector, Macedonia, September 1918

On 9 October 1915 company-sized scout (*Esploratori*) units were established for trench missions, foreunners of the *Arditi* assault units of 5 July 1917. This junior NCO wears the standard Other Ranks' grey-green (*grigio-verde*) service and field uniform introduced 22 September 1909. He wears *Cagliari* Brigade collar patches; shoulder welt company number; and cuff rank chevrons introduced March 1917. On the right sleeve he has the scout's badge, and on the left the qualified marksman's and grenade throwers' badges above a field promotion crown. His French M1915 Adrian helmet, issued 24 April 1916, has a grey-green cover with a black-stencilled crown and regimental number; he wears the M1907 grey-green leather belt with first model *Arditi* dagger, ammunition pouches, canvas haversack and Polivalente Z gasmask introduced January 1917. He carries a 6.5mm Fucile M91 rifle and a SIPE hand grenade.

E2: Sergent, 2bis Zouave Regiment, French 11th Colonial Infantry Division; Monastir Sector, Macedonia, May 1917

This NCO wears the standard Other Ranks' khaki service and field uniform introduced in 1915 for units recruited outside Metropolitan France. The M1915 greatcoat has dark red branch-colour collar patch cyphers, gold field uniform cuff rank insignia, and two dark brown service chevrons (one year plus six months) on the left upper sleeve. The M1915 tunic underneath had the same badges. He wears the red *chechia* Zouave cap, M1915 black leather equiment, and carries an 8mm Lebel 86/93 bolt-action rifle.

E3: Shtabs Kapitan, Russian 2nd Brigade; Monastir Sector, Macedonia, May 1917

This officer wears the officers' khaki wool service and field uniform introduced 10 March 1909. His tunic, cut like the M1907 but with horn buttons instead of metal, has gold

service uniform reversible rank shoulder boards (the khaki field side was usually hidden) and two button-colour left cuff wound stripes (introduced 5 December 1916). He wears the M1911 version of the *Moskovskiy* (Moscow) Life Guard Infantry regimental breast badge – the officer's original regiment; and the Cross of the Order of St.Vladimir with Swords 3rd Class. His peaked cap has the black-gold officers' cockade. He wears officers' M1912 brown leather equipment with double shoulder braces, M1895 Nagant 7.62mm revolver, and an M1909 Golden Sword, awarded for bravery, with a St.George's pommel badge and black-orange sword knot.

F: BULGARIAN ARMY

F1: Rotmister, 3rd Grand Duchess Maria Krilova Cavalry Regiment, 1st Cavalry Division; Macedonia, February 1916

This officer wears the standard Bulgarian officers' M1908 service and field uniform. His M1908 light grey hooded double-breasted greatcoat has branch collar and cuff piping and collar patches – dark blue for cavalry, red for general officers, otherwise dark green – and grey-green M1915 field shoulder boards with his regiment's honorary colonel's monogram. The grey-green peaked cap has a branch-colour cap band and pipings and the standard white-green-red national cockade. He also wears a grey-green service tunic with collar and cuff piping, grey-green (dark blue for cavalry) branch-colour piped breeches (general officers had double crimson, general staff officers double red stripes), riding boots with spurs, brown leather equipment and binocular case, and a black holster for his M1895 Nagant revolver. The M1915 officers' plain peaked cap had a black leather or grey-green narrow braided chin strap, the M1915 tunic no cuff-piping. From 1915 German field-grey uniforms began to replace Bulgarian grey-green.

F2: Feldfebel, 4th Crown Prince Boris Artillery Regiment, 4th 'Preslav' Infantry Division; Dobrudja, September 1916

This battery sergeant major wears the Other Ranks' M1908 'tobacco-brown' service and field uniform with round artillery cuffs. His tunic has artillery-red collar and strap pipings; NCOs' gold collar, cuff and strap braid; regimental monogram, and left sleeve re-enlistment chevrons. He has a

Brigadier Berthelot and a French captain, both dressed in the French M1915 horizon-blue service uniform (note Berthelot's double dark blue general officers' trouser stripes) and a French lieutenant (4th right with sword) awarding medals to troops of the Rumanian 1st Army, summer 1917. The Rumanian officer (2nd right), is wearing the rarely worn M1916 service dress tunic (probably in horizon blue) with corps-colour collar (1st Corps – yellow; 2nd – white; 3rd – dark green; 4th – blue; 5th – red) omitting collar rank chevrons, with black trousers. The officer saluting wears an M1912 field service tunic with non-standard pleated patch pockets, a black mourning armband, the M1916 *Mihai Viteazul* (Michael the Brave) gallantry medal, and a leather binoculars case; the officer (5th right) wears an M1916 field tunic, and the officer (1st left) has his shirt collar folded over his M1912 field tunic collar – a common affectation. (Horia Serbanescu Collection)

Cap badges are worn on the M1910 officers' peaked service cap and all ranks' peakless field cap; badges with the pre-28 August 1910 crown of the Principality of Montenegro are still worn. M1910 officers' shoulder boards are worn on the M1910 service and field tunic, M1914 service tunic and greatcoat. All Ranks have gold buttons, Other Ranks wear plain khaki shoulder straps (branch-colour woollen bars prescribed for NCOs were never worn). General officers (*generali*) **(1-4)**:- gold metal cap badges; gold Russian braid shoulder boards piped crimson, silver braid or metal stars. Field and subaltern officers (*oficiri*) **(5-9)**:- gold metal cap badges (5-8) (silver scimitars - 7; silver eagle, lion, shield - 8), silver metal cap badge (9); gold braid shoulder boards piped branch-colour, silver metal stars.

Standard-bearers (*barjaktari*) **(10-13)**:- gold metal cap-badges (10-12) (silver cross - 12), silver metal cap-badge (13). Non-commissioned officers (*podoficiri*) **(14-15)** and men (*vojnici*) **(16-18)**:- white metal cap badges. Branch colours:- General officers - crimson; king's adjutants - white; infantry (including recce) - scarlet; Royal Guard - special uniform; machine gun companies - light blue; artillery - orange (black M1914 tunic collars); engineers - blue; signals - green; medical and administrative officials - silver/ black braid shoulder-boards, red/gold cockades.

1. Vrhovni Komandant *(Field Marshal)*
2. Glavni inspektor *(Lt. Gen.)*
3. Divizijar *(Maj. Gen.)*
4. Brigadir *(Brigadier)* King's Adjutant
5. Komandir *(Lt. Col.)* Infantry
6. Komandir *(Lt. Col.)* Artillery
7. Kapetan *(Captain)* Staff
8. Porucnik *(Lieutenant)* MG companies
9. Potporucnik *(Lieutenant)* Engineers
10. Alajbarjaktar *(Ensign of the Army)*
11. Brigadni barjaktar *(Brigade Ensign)*
12. Bataljonski barjaktar *(Battalion Ensign)*
13. Cetni barjaktar *(Company Ensign)*
14. Vodnik *(Sergeant)*
15. Desecar *(Corporal)*
16. Perjanik *(Private)* Royal Guard
17. Topnik *(Private)* Artillery
18. Vojnik *(Private)* Other branches

Notes 1 King Nikola I only. 2 Crown Prince Danilo only. 5 Principality crown. 6 All artillery officers (6-9) and NCOs (14-15) added cannons and cannon-balls as illustrated. 14 *Topovodja* in the artillery.

black artillery cap and cap-band with red piping and Other Ranks' national cockade, standard black belt and riding boots, spurs and revolver. Other Ranks of élite infantry and cavalry regiments (with shoulder strap monograms) wore the M1908 officers' style grey-green uniform with regimental front edge piping.

F3: Efreytor, 34th Infantry Regiment, 9th 'Pleven' Infantry Division; Battle of Doiran, September 1918

This soldier wears the standard Other Ranks' M1915 field-grey infantry service and field uniform with concealed breast pockets and pointed infantry cuffs, later also manufactured with lower pockets only and plain cuffs. The peaked cap is plain; the tunic has a red-piped collar, front edge, cuff and shoulder strap piping, with a red cloth rank loop and regimental number. Troops wore Bulgarian-style civilian *opanci* shoes and socks in dry weather, black marching boots in wet. He has M1908 black leather infantry equipment and has his hooded M1915 single-breasted greatcoat rolled around the backpack. He carries an Austro-Hungarian 8mm Mannlicher M1895 infantry rifle.

G: GREEK ARMY

G1: Lochagos, Arkhipelagos Division, National Defence Corps; Skrá di Legen, Struma Sector, Macedonia, May 1918

On 10 June 1910 the Greek Army adopted a superior quality khaki wool service and field uniform for officers and warrant officers. The kepi had a national cockade, button-colour wire crown and between one and six gold cap band rank rings (general officers – gold braid chin strap and cap band); the tunic had a stand-up collar, round cuffs, concealed pockets and branch-colour collar, cuff and front edge pipings. On 1 August 1915 a German-style peaked cap (general officers, gold chin strap and cap band) was introduced with the tunic illustrated, with branch-colour buttoned collar patches (general officers, gold braid piped red). On 28 October 1916 the Provisional Government reinstated the kepi with dark brown braid rank rings (general officers, 3-1 dark brown braid oak wreaths and gold chin-strap). This lieutenant has breeches and infantry officers' leather leggings; three left sleeve gold officers' service chevrons for 18 months' front line service, and two right sleeve gold officers' wound

M1908 shoulder boards are worn on the M1908 grey-green officers' or tobacco-brown Other Ranks' field tunic, or the M1915 grey-green officers' or Other Ranks' field tunic. The Life Guards have special ceremonial shoulder knots. General officers (*generali*) (1-3):- gold russian-braid boards, gold buttons, red piping, silver metal pips. Cavalry (2) - silver russian braid, silver buttons, gold pips. M1915 boards - grey-green russian braid, red piping, gold/silver pips and buttons. Field officers (*shtabofitseri*) (4,6,7) and subaltern officers (*oberofitseri*) (8,9,11):- gold russian-braid boards, gold buttons, branch piping, 1-2 facing-cloth centre stripes, silver metal pips and unit/branch insignia. Cavalry (6) - silver zigzag braid, silver buttons, gold pips and unit/branch insignia; (9) gold zigzag braid, silver buttons, silver pips and unit insignia. M1915 boards - grey-green cloth, branch piping, facing-cloth centre stripes, gold/silver pips and buttons. NCOs (*Podofitseri*) (12,13,16) and men (*Redovi*) (17,18):- facing-cloth shoulder boards, gold buttons, branch piping, yellow wool edging, bars and unit/branch insignia (gold braid for 13). Cavalry (16) - silver buttons, white wool edging, bars and unit/branch insignia (silver braid for 13). M1915 boards - grey-green, gold buttons, branch piping, red braid edging and bars. Life Guard Regiment (5,10,15):- Silver cords, gold pips. NCOs and Men (15) - white cords and rank knots.

1. General ot Pechotata (*General*) Infantry
2. General-Leytenant (*Lt. Gen.*) Cavalry
3. General-Mayor (*Maj. Gen.*) Infantry (M1915)
4. Polkovnik (*Colonel*) 3rd Infantry Regt.
5. Polkovnik (*Colonel*) Life Guard Regt.
6. Podpolkovnik (*Lt. Col.*) 1st Cavalry Regt.
7. Mayor (*Major*) General Staff (M1915)
8. Sanitaren Kapitan (*Captain*) Medical Corps
9. Poruchik (*Lieutenant*) 4th Cavalry Regt.
10. Poruchik (*Lieutenant*) Life Guard Regt.
11. Podporuchik (*2nd Lieutenant*) 10th Engineer Bn (M1915)
12. Ofitserski kandidat (*Acting 2nd Lt.*) 5th Artillery Regt.
13. Feldfebel (*W.O. II*) 2nd Mountain Infantry Regt.
14. Starshi Feyerwerker (*Sergeant*) Horse Artillery (M1915)
15. Starshi Podofitser (*Sergeant*) Life Guard Regt.
16. Mladshi Podofitser (*Corporal*) 3rd Cavalry Regt.
17. Efreytor (Lance-Corporal) 3rd Cavalry Regt. (M1915)
18. Rednik (*Private*) 21st Infantry Regt.

Notes 1 Cavalry - 'General ot Konnitsata'; Artillery - 'General ot Artilleriata'. 8 Cavalry - 'Rotmister'; in other branches 'Kapitan'. 13 Cavalry - 'Vachmister'. 14 Artillery - 'Starshi Podofitser' in other branches. 15 Military Police - 'Starshi strayar'. 16 Artillery - 'Mladshi Feyerverker'; Military Police - 'Mladshi strayar'. 17 Artillery - 'Bombardir'. 18 Artillery - 'Kanonir'.

chevrons, both introduced 14 January 1918; and a British Sam Browne belt and holster. The khaki sidecap (introduced 4 January 1918), with cockade, crown and dark brown braid rank chevrons, is tucked in his belt.

G2: Lochias, 2/39 Evzone Regiment, 3rd Division; Vetrenik, Crna Sector, Macedonia, September 1918

This NCO wears the M1908 Evzone Other Ranks' khaki three-quarter *doulama* tunic with M1868 rank stripes. Following the order of 4 August 1914 he has replaced infantry-red shoulder straps with khaki but retained the collar and cuff piping – buttonless infantry collar patches were added on 1 August 1915. He wears the *fustanella* skirt, long woollen socks, garters and *tsarouchia* mountain boots, although infantry trousers and puttees were also worn. Usually the black tassel was removed in combat from his M1908 Evzone fez with national cockade and yellow (button-colour) crown. He wears M1908 brown leather equipment and waterbottle, and carries an M1903 Austro-Hungarian Schönauer 6.5mm rotary magazine rifle. Evzone officers wore standard infantry uniform.

G3: Ypodekaneus, 2nd Cavalry Regiment, 2nd Corps; Doiran Sector, Macedonia, September 1918

This trooper wears the Other Ranks' khaki wool service and field uniform, introduced on 28 June 1908 with a branch-colour collar and cuff pipings and shoulder straps, modified on 1 August 1915 with buttonless branch-colour collar patches replacing pipings and plain khaki shoulder straps. He wears the French M1915 Adrian helmet introduced 1917 with the Greek national badge. The M1908 khaki peaked cap with national cockade and white (button-colour) crown was replaced by the M1910 kepi with branch-coloured crown piping; by the peaked cap again on 1 August 1915; and the kepi on 28 October 1916. He has three silver NCOs' sleeve service chevrons (privates, black wool) for 18 months' front line service; cavalry breeches and riding boots, and M1908 brown leather cavalry ammunition pouches; a short M1903 Schönauer 6.5mm cavalry carbine and M1887 sword. Dismounted personnel wore long khaki trousers, replaced in 1915 by trousers and puttees.

43

Branch	Officers' shoulder-board braid [1]	Greatcoat collar-patch	Facing cloth [4]	Piping cloth [5]	Unit number, badge or monogram on shoulder-board
Infantry and artillery generals	gold russian	black	red	red	-
Cavalry generals	silver russian	black	scarlet	red	-
General Staff officers	silver russian	black velvet	black velvet	red	-
1st Prince Alexander Infantry Rgt.	gold russian	red	red	red	crown, A
4th Crown Prince Boris Infantry Rgt.	gold russian	light red	light red	light red	crown, B
5th Duke Robert of Parma Infantry Rgt.	gold russian	red	red	red	crown, RP
6th King Ferdinand Infantry Rgt.	gold russian	white	white	white	crown, Ø
8th Princess Maria Luisa Infantry Rgt.	gold russian	dark blue	dark blue	dark blue	crown, ML
9th Princess Clementina Infantry Rgt.	gold russian	blue cloth	blue cloth	blue cloth	crown, K
17th Grand Duke Vladimir Infantry Rgt	gold russian	cherry red	cherry red	cherry red	crown, E
18th King Ferdinand Infantry Rgt.	gold russian	green-blue	green-blue	green-blue	crown, Ø
20th Prince Kyril Infantry Rgt.	gold russian	red	red	red	crown, K
22nd Duke Karl-Edvard Infantry Rgt.	gold russian	light green	light green	light green	crown, KE
72 numbered infantry regiments	gold russian	red	red	red	2, 3, 7, 10 - 16, 19, 21, 23 – 82
3 Mountain infantry regiments	gold russian	red	red	red	(∏ / 1-3
21 Frontier Guard companies	gold russian	red	red	red	(∏.C
Royal Life Guard Cavalry Rgt.	silver cords	scarlet	-	-	small crown, (Ø
1st King Ferdinand Cavalry Rgt.	silver zig-zag	scarlet	scarlet	white	crown, (Ø
2nd Princess Maria Luisa Cavalry Rgt	silver zig-zag	scarlet	scarlet	red	crown, ML
3rd Grand Duchess Maria Krilova Cav. Rgt.	silver zig-zag	scarlet	scarlet	yellow	crown, M
4th Crown Prince Boris Cavalry Rgt.	gold zig-zag	raspberry	raspberry	white	crown, B
Six numbered cavalry regiments	silver zig-zag	scarlet	scarlet	white	5 – 10
2 horse artillery regiments	gold russian	black [2]	black [2/3]	red	AK
3rd Crown Prince Boris Artillery Rgt.	gold russian	black [2]	black [2/3]	red	crown, B
4th King Ferdinand Artillery Rgt.	gold russian	black [2]	black [2/3]	red	crown, (Ø
11 divisional artillery regiments.	gold russian	black [2]	black [2/3]	red	1 – 2, 5 – 13
3 Heavy Artillery battalions	gold russian	black [2]	black [2/3]	red	T
3 Garrison Artillery battalions	gold russian	black [2]	black [2/3]	red	K
3 Mountain Artillery battalions	gold russian	black [2]	black [2/3]	red	∏
13 divisional Engineer battalions	silver russian	black [2]	black [2/3]	red	1 – 13
1 Railway Battalion	silver russian	black [2]	black [2/3]	red	winged wheel
1 Bridging Engineer Battalion	silver russian	black [2]	black [2/3]	red	fouled anchor
1 Signals Battalion	silver russian	black [2]	black [2/3]	red	lightning flashes
Air Corps		original branch			
13 Military Police companies (mounted)	silver zig-zag	red	red	red	red aiguillettes
13 Military Police companies (dismounted)	gold russian	red	red	red	red aiguillettes
Medical officers	silver russian	black velvet	black velvet	black	cup, snakes
13 medical companies other ranks	white braid	black	red	red	-
Veterinary officers	silver russian	black velvet	black velvet	black	snake
Pharmaceutical officers	silver russian	black velvet	black velvet	black	goblet

Notes

1 As worn in service dress. Officers' rank pips are gold on silver braid, silver on gold braid. 2 Velvet for officers, cloth for NCOs and men. 3 Centre-stripes on field and subaltern -officers' M1908 and M1915 shoulder boards are red. 4 Cap-band of the M1908 officers' and other ranks' peaked cap; centre-stripes on field and subaltern officers' M1908 and M1915 shoulder boards (except under footnote 3); M1908 other ranks' collar and shoulder-straps. 5 Piping on:- the cap-band and crown of the M1908 officers' and other ranks' peaked-cap; the M1908 officers' and other ranks' greatcoat collar-patch, collar and cuff; M1908 officers', M1908 and M1915 other ranks', tunic collar and cuffs; M1908 officers' shoulder-boards, other ranks' M1908 and M1915 shoulder-straps.

H: RUMANIAN ARMY

H1: Fruntas, 74th Reserve Infantry Regiment, 15th Infantry Division; First Battle of Oituz, Western Moldavia, October 1916

On 4 February 1912 the Rumanian Army adopted a grey-green service and field uniform. This infantryman wears the Other Ranks' *capela* field cap with branch-colour pipings and regimental number. His Other Ranks' greatcoat has branch-colour spearhead collar patches and shoulder strap regimental numbers. He wears high-shaft ankle boots with branch-colour piped breeches confined by puttees, which in 1915 replaced the trousers with integral anklets. He has M1891 leather equipment and carries a standard 6.5mm M1893 Mannlicher bolt-action rifle.

M1910 officers' and warrant officers' shoulder boards (introduced 16 March 1910) are worn on the M1910 and M1915 khaki service tunic. NCOs and men wear M1910 shoulder straps on the M1908 khaki service tunic and M1915 shoulder straps (introduced 1 August 1915) on the M1915 khaki service tunic. General officers *(Avioteroi)* (1-3):- gold Russian-braid board, gold button, red piping, large silver woven stars. Officers *(Axiomatikoi)* (4-6):- two button-colour lace stripes on branch-colour shoulder board, medium reverse button-colour woven stars. (7-9):- one button-colour lace stripe on branch-colour shoulder boards, medium reverse button-colour woven stars. NCOs *(Ypaxiomatikoi)* and men *(Hoplites)* (10-18):- one button-colour lace stripe on branch-colour shoulder board. (11-12):- branch-colour shoulderb strap, black thread unit insignia. (13):- khaki shoulder strap. (14-17) - button-colour M1868 20mm (7mm for 17) lace stripes with branch-colour piping on both cuffs; (18) No rank insignia. M1910 Branch colours (M1915 in brackets):- Line, Cretan and Evzone Infantry, General Staff - red; Cavalry - crimson (green); Artillery - bright red (black); Engineers, Air Corps - blue (cherry red); Supply - bright red (raspberry red); Ordnance - bright red (chocolate-brown); Medical, Veterinary officers - crimson velvet; Medical other ranks - red (crimson); Pharmacist officers - green velvet; Pay Corps - orange; Gendarmerie - dark blue. Cavalry, Supply, Engineers and Gendarmerie have silver buttons and lace, other branches gold.

1. Stratigos *(General)*
2. Antistratigos *(Lt. Gen.)*
3. Ypostratigos *(Maj. Gen.)*
4. Syntagmatarchis *(Colonel)* Cavalry
5. Antisyntag-matarchis *(Lt. Col.)* Infantry
6. Tagmatarchis *(Major)* Artillery
7. Iatros *(Captain)* Medical Corps
8. Ypolochagos *(Lieutenant)* Evzone Infantry
9. Anthypolochagos *(2nd Lieutenant)* Engineers
10. Anthypaspistis *(WOII)* Ordnance
11. NCOs & Men Infantry
12. NCOs & Men Artillery
13. NCOs & Men (M 1915)
14. Enimotarchis A. *(Colour Sergeant)* Gendarmerie
15. Lochias *(Sergeant)* Infantry
16. Dekaneus *(Corporal)* (M1915) Supply
17. Ypodekaneus *(Lance-Corporal)* Artillery
18. Stratiotis *(Private)* Cavalry

Notes 1 Rank held by King Constantine I (1913-1917) and King Alexander (1917-1920). 7 Cavalry - Ilarchos; Veterinary - Kteniatros; Pharmacist - Farmakopeos; Gendarmerie - Moiarchos. Other branches - Lochagos - Yplarchos; Medical - Ypiatros; Veterinary - Ypokteniatros; Pharmacist - Ypofarmakopeos; Gendarmerie - Ypomoiarchos. 9 Cavalry - Anthypilarchos; Medical - Anthypiatros; Pharmacist - Anthypofarmakopeos; Gendarmerie - Anthypomoiarchos. 14 Other branches - Epilochias. 15 Gendarmerie - Enomotarchis B. 16 Gendarmerie - Archifilax. 17 Gendarmerie (lowest rank) - Chorofilax (no insignia).

H2: Sergent major, 3rd Light Infantry Regiment, 5th Infantry Division; Battle of Marasesti, Western Moldavia, August 1917

The M1912 Other Ranks' grey-green field tunic had external unpleated pockets with squared flaps; spearhead collar patches (horn badges for light infantry), shoulder strap unit numbers, collar and shoulder strap piping were in branch colours. In 1915 the pockets became internal and pipings were abolished, and by 1917 tunic and breeches were in the brownish undyed wool illustrated. He has the French M1915 Adrian helmet painted grey-blue (or black) with royal monogram, issued in January 1917; grey-blue puttees; Italian M1907 equipment; the *Virtutea Militara* Medal 1st Class, and an M1893 Mannlicher rifle.

H3: Locotenent-colonel, 11th Artillery Regiment, 6th Infantry Division; Western Moldavia, November 1918

On 5 May 1916 French-supplied 'horizon blue' uniforms were introduced but effectively only reached officers. This officer wears the M1916 tunic; the M1912 grey-green tunic had internal pockets with scalloped flaps and a fly-front. His kepi, the M1912 model in grey-blue, has the national cockade and royal monogram (general officers, a gold star on a silver sun). He has M1912 black breeches for general officers, cavalry, artillery and frontier guard officers, with branch-colour piping (general officers, double red stripes) and artillery officers' riding boots (cavalry added a gold metal rosette). Other branches had grey-green breeches with brown leather gaiters and ankle boots, and in 1916 all branches had grey-blue breeches.

M1912 shoulder boards and shoulder straps were worn on the M1912 grey-green field tunic, M1915 Other Ranks' and M1916 officers' bluish-grey field tunic, and the M1917 Other Ranks' brown field tunic. General officers *(generali)* **(1-3)**:- gold braid boards, gold buttons, red piping, silver metal bars. Field officers *(ofiteri superiori)* **(4-6)**:- uniform strap, gold buttons, gold centre stripe, branch-colour piping, silver metal bars. Subaltern officers *(ofiteri inferiori)* **(7-9)**:- uniform strap, gold buttons, branch-colour piping, silver metal bars. Non-commissioned officers *(Subofiteri)* **(10-12)**:- uniform strap (branch-colour piping on M1915 tunic), branch-colour unit insignia, black buttons, gold braid bars. Senior privates *(Graduati)* **(13-15)**:- uniform strap, black buttons, branch-colour unit insignia, gold braid (13) or yellow wool bars. Privates *(Soldati)* **(15-16)**:- uniform strap (branch-colour piping on M1915 tunic), black buttons, branch-colour unit insignia.

1. General de corp de armata *(General)*
2. General de divizie *(Lt. Gen.)*
3. General de brigada *(Maj. Gen.)*
4. Colonel *(Colonel)* Infantry
5. Locotenent-colonel *(Lt. Col.)* General Staff
6. Maior *(Major)* 5th Line Cavalry Regt..
7. Capitan *(Captain)* Field Artillery
8. Locotenent *(Lieutenant)* Engineers
9. Sublocotenent *(2nd Lieutenant)* Territorial Cavalry
10. Plutonier major *(Col. Sergeant)* 1st Infantry Regt.
11. Plutonier *(Sergeant)* 4th Line Cavalry Regt.
12. Sergent major *(Lance-Sergeant)* 10th Engineer Bn.
13. Sergent *(Corporal)* Air Corps
14. Caporal *(Lance-Corporal)* 9th Light Inf. Regt..
15. Fruntas *(Senior Private)* 2nd Calarasi. Regt..
16. Soldat *(Private)* 11th Artillery Regt.

Medical officers had ranks *medic general 3 - medic sublocotenent 9*; supply officers, *intendent general 3 - adjunct clasa II 7*, with gold metal rank bars. Veterinary officers had ranks *veterinar colonel 4 - veterinar sublocotenent 9*; pharmacist officers, *farmacist colonel 4 - farmacist sublo- cotenent 9*. Military Police officers had silver metal rank bars, NCOs silver braid rank bars. Administrative officers had ranks *administrator principal 6 - administrator class III 9* with gold metal rank bars and *subofiter clasa I 10, subofiter clasa II 11* with silver braid bars. 14 Cavalry and Artillery - *Brigadier.*

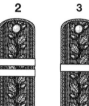

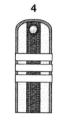
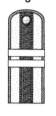

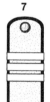

LEFT **Soldiers of the *Armée de l'Orient* pose in a photograph dated 10 December 1917. (Back row, left to right): an Italian artilleryman in M1907 field cap and tunic, a Greek private in an M1918 field cap and greatcoat, and a Serb private in M1908 field cap and greatcoat. (Front row, left to right): a British cavalryman in M1902 uniform with distinctive shoulder bandolier; a Russian private in M1907 khaki *gymnastiorka* field tunic, and a French private in M1915 'horizon blue' field kepi and greatcoat. (Kraljevo Museum)**

OPPOSITE **Pasrt of a group of Montenegrin reserve officers, mainly captains commanding companies, besieging Shkodër in March 1913, with uniforms still worn in the Great War. They are wearing M1910 uniforms with khaki pillbox field caps with the obsolete large M1871 rank cap badges retained by the Reserve Army, and no shoulder boards. Note the plain cloak worn by the officer (rear, left) and the officer's sword suspended by shoulder belt. As in so many photographs of Balkan troops, most have moustaches. (Dusan Babac Collection)**

Branch and unit distinctions of the Rumanian Army
15 August 1916 - 11 November 1918

Branch	Collar-patch	Piping	Other ranks' cap and shoulder-strap insignia in piping colour
General-officers	bright red	bright red	n/a
General Staff officers	original branch, white lightning	original branch	n/a
40 Line Infantry (dorobanti) regiments	bright red	bright red	1 - 40
40 Reserve (reserva) Infantry regiments	bright red	bright red	41 - 80
10 Light Infantry (vinatori) regiments	dark green/green horn	dark green	horn (cap); 1 - 10 (strap)
1 Mountain Infantry Regiment	dark green	dark green	V.M
1 Frontier Guard (Graniceri) Brigade	light green piped yellow	light green	G.r
Royal Bodyguard (Escorta) Regiment	black	black	R.E
1st Line Cavalry (Rosiori) Regiment	yellow	yellow	1
2nd Line Cavalry Regiment	white	white	2
3rd Line Cavalry Regiment	dark green	dark green	3
4th Line Cavalry Regiment	light blue	light blue	crown, M
5th Line Cavalry Regiment	light green	light green	crown, H/II
6th Line Cavalry Regiment	blue	blue	6
7th Line Cavalry Regiment	coffee brown	coffee brown	7
8th Line Cavalry Regiment	mauve	mauve	8
9th Line Cavalry Regiment	pink	pink	9
10th Line Cavalry Regiment	light grey	light grey	10
11th Line Cavalry Regiment	dark red	dark red	11
12th Line Cavalry Regiment	violet	violet	12
10 Cavalry (Calarasi) Regts	bright red piped black	bright red	1 - 10
30 Divisional Field Artillery Regiments	black velvet[1]	black	1 - 30 (strap); cap adds cannons
2 Divisional Horse Artillery Battalions	black velvet[1]	black	1 - 2 D.C (strap); cap adds cannons
2 Garrison Artillery Brigades	black velvet[1]	black	1C - 2C (strap); cap adds cannons
Armoured Car Corps	black velvet[1]	black	C.A
15 Divisional Engineer Battalions	black velvet[1] piped bright red	black	1 - 15
15 Divisional Signal Companies	black velvet[1] piped bright red	black	1 - 15
1 Railway Engineer Battalion	black velvet[1] piped bright red	black	C.F
1 Bridging Engineer Battalion	black velvet[1] piped bright red	black	anchor
1 Garrison Engineer Battalion	black velvet[1] piped bright red	black	P.C
1 Specialist Engineer Battalion	black velvet[1] piped bright red	black	C.S
1 Balloon Battalion	black velvet[1] piped bright red	black	A.e
10 Air Corps squadrons	black velvet[1] piped bright red	black	A.v
15 Div. M.P. (Jandarmi) companies	white	white	1 - 5
Medical officers	black velvet piped blue	black velvet	-
15 Div. Medical companies (other ranks)	red	red	1 - 15 & red cross
Veterinary officers	violet velvet piped bright violet	violet velvet	-
Pharmacist Officers	green velvet piped light green	green velvet	-
15 Div. Supply (Intendenta) Columns	bright red piped white	bright red	1-15
Administrative Officers & NCOs	bright red piped white	bright red	-

Note [1] Officers had black velvet, other ranks had black cloth.

INDEX

Figures in **bold** refer to illustrations